Freezer-Friendly DUMP DINNERS

60 SCRUMPTIOUS MAKE-AHEAD MEALS THAT PRACTICALLY COOK THEMSELVES!

ERIN CHASE

© 2018 by Erin Chase & FreezEasy Media.

All rights reserved worldwide. No portion of this book may be reproduced in any manner without written permission except for brief quotations in critical reviews or articles.

Published by FreezEasy Media, via CreateSpace.

ISBN 10: 717212352
ISBN 13: 978-1717212351

Limit of Liability/Disclaimer of Warranty: The Company and author make no representations or warranties with respect to the accuracy of completeness of the contents of this work and specifically disclaim all warranties, including without limitation warranties of fitness for a particular purpose. No warranty may be created or extended by sales or promotional materials. The advice and strategies contained herein may not be suitable for every situation. The work is sold with the understanding that the company and author is not engaged in rendering medical, legal or other professional advice or services. Neither the company nor author shall be liable for damages arising herefrom. Finally, readers should be aware that Internet websites listed in this work may have changed or disappeared between when this work was written and when it is read.

Always follow safety and common-sense cooking protocol while using kitchen utensils, operating ovens or stoves, as well as electric pressure cookers, and handling uncooked food. If children are assisting in the preparation of any recipe, they should be supervised by an adult.

Instant Pot is a registered trademark of Double Insights, Inc. and the name is used in the recipe titles in this cookbook. FreezEasy is a registered trademark of FreezEasy Media.

For general information about our workshops, products and services, or to obtain technical support, please contact our Customer Care Team at support@freezeasy.com.

For more great recipes and resources, visit www.myfreezeasy.com.

FREE ONLINE WORKSHOP

Want to spend less time in the kitchen, and more time enjoying other things in life? Need dinner to "take care of itself"? Want to personalize and customize a freezer meal plan - with recipes your family will love?

MyFreezEasy will do all the heavy lifting for you! In a matter of seconds, our apps will pull together your freezer meal recipes, shopping lists, step-by-step instructions and printable labels for your meals. Load up your freezer with make-ahead meals and dinnertime will be a breeze.

In this free online workshop, you'll learn just about everything you need to know about freezer cooking and how it can transform your family's dinner experience.

Sign up for free at: www.myfreezeasy.com/workshop

TABLE OF CONTENTS

About Dump Dinners — 5

How Freezer Cooking Helps Me Survive This Busy Mom Life — 8

Other General Freezer Cooking Hacks — 10

Dump Dinners Recipes — 12

Freezer Meal Plan #1 — 72

Freezer Meal Plan #1 — 84

More Freezer Cooking Resources from Erin — 96

About Dump Dinners

Do you find yourself running through the drive thru often? Because it's "fast and simple"? Maybe because you don't have to think too much about it? Or perhaps it's that you just can't decide what to fix for supper, so you end up calling into the speaker - "I'd like a #2 with cheese and a Sprite. Also, a #8, 8 count with sweet tea. And a kid's meal, 4 count..."

You know how it goes.

It goes like that, but going that way is expensive, not so healthy for you (usually!), and really doesn't save as much time as you think. Because there are meals that have hands-on time of less than the amount of time you'd spend just sitting in the drive thru. We'll forget about the you also spend time getting to the drive thru and getting home. Lump all that time together and you could easily get a meal together for your dinner table!

In fact, I could put together 6 of these "dump dinners" in the same amount of time that you sit in some drive thrus. Seriously - because some drive thru lanes are SLOW, and these meals are FAST.

What is this "dump dinner" thing I'm referring to?!

A "dump dinner" is a dinner where you quickly dump ingredients together into a baggie or tray, to prepare for the freezer. Then, the meal is easy to thaw and get cooking.

It's fast both on the "prep for the freezer" side, as well as the "cook for dinner" side.

Here's what a "dump dinner" prep and cooking looks like in my kitchen:

To prepare the meals for the freezer, I'll set up several of our "bag holders" and add the plastic freezer storage bags to the clips. (See bag holders at ShopFreezEasy.com!)

With the bags being held open for me, I can easily add ingredients to the baggies, then remove air and seal up for the freezer. Here's an example of ingredients that I would dump in:

- 3-4 small boneless, skinless chicken breasts
- 15 oz. can diced tomatoes
- 15 oz. can black beans
- 1 cup salsa
- 2 Tbsp taco seasoning

The only "prep work" involved with a Salsa Chicken recipe, like the one listed above, is opening the cans. The recipes in this Dump Dinners Cookbook from MyFreezEasy have little to no "prep work" at all. You might open some cans or slice an onion, but that's about it.

Once these ingredients have been added to the baggie or disposable baking tray, you can remove air and seal or cover with foil. We recommend making sure that all the ingredients are at room temperature or cooler, to prevent increased risk of freezer burn.

To cook these "dump dinners" for dinner, you'll need to take it out of the freezer, thaw the contents of the baggie or tray and then cook as directed. To quickly thaw the meal, you can place into a large bowl of warm water or larger baking dish of warm water and let it soak in the water for a few minutes.

Once partially thawed*, you can add the contents of the baggie to the slow cooker, electric pressure cooker, or other cookware. To get the example Salsa Chicken recipe cooking, I would add it to my slow cooker, as is, and cook on low for 8 hours. An alternative cooking method would be using the electric pressure cooker by adding the frozen contents of the meal plus 1 cup of water or chicken stock, then cooking on High Pressure for 25 minutes. It will both thaw out and cook in the slow cooker or electric pressure cooker, using the times indicated.

*Note: For grilled meals and seafood meals, we recommend thawing completely before cooking as directed by the recipe.

Many of the dump dinners included in this cookbook are cooked in the slow cooker or electric pressure cooker, which is why this example is being highlighted here. Other recipes will have specific appropriate directions for cooking after being frozen.

Dump Ingredients Together - Seal and Freeze - Thaw and Cook.

Do you see now how these meals will help keep you out of the drive thru?!

It's the fastest way to get a bunch of meals prepared for your freezer. **Dump Dinners are the VERY BEST way to do "fast food at home."**

No more drive thru for you. Well, at least, I hope it's less drive thru for you.

With a few minutes prep before freezing, and a few minutes to thaw and cook, dinner has never been so easy, and inexpensive too!

How Freezer Cooking Helps Me Survive This Busy Mom Life

Freezer cooking and the "fast food at home" philosophy of MyFreezEasy has saved me from the drive thru - take out - dining out temptation on dozens (hundreds!?) of occasions! I'm not opposed to the drive thru or take out or dining out, but I do think those meals out on the town should be planned and part of your budget. Getting dump dinners and other meals into the freezer has helped keep me out of the drive thru and eating more meals at home that are healthier and more frugal.

Recently, I found myself at the pediatrician's office with the last appointment of the day. I generally have a 'no last appointment of the morning or afternoon' policy with doctor's offices, because you end up waiting while they catch up from falling behind throughout their visits. But that was the only slot I could get that day for a son whom I suspected had strep throat.

So I'm still sitting in the waiting room at 4:50pm, waiting to see the doctor. At that point, I knew it would be 6pm before we got home, and I'm normally in the kitchen from 5 - 6 pm to prep dinner or reheat a freezer meal. That particular day, I was starting to worry. The temptation to hit the local burger joint on my way home was getting stronger. And just as I was adding up what that drive thru bill might cost, my husband texted that he was on his way home from work.

PHEW! I quickly texted back and asked if he'd be able to get dinner going in the skillet. He said he didn't have anything pressing when he got home, so I shot back the play-by-play on how to thaw and reheat some sloppy joe meat from the freezer.

When I finally arrived home after the strep test (it was positive) and buzzing through to pick up the prescription, it was 6pm. And it smelled amazing in the house, and I just scooped together some sloppy joes, cut up some fruit, grabbed some chips and dinner was served. Total cost of the meal was probably around $5-$6 for all of us. (I'm a ninja sale and deals grocery shopper!)

I was able to save dinner that night, without having to spend $40 in the drive thru!

Another example comes from this past flu season. In 2018, the flu season was exceptionally rough and it hit our family twice - once with each strain. We ended up having a sick kid home from school and activities for 7 weeks in a row, with a brief reprieve in between the 2 strains.

I did my best to keep the sick ones quarantined, keep the house clean and disinfected, plus the time and energy spent nursing them back to health - I was exhausted. There was little energy left for dinner.

It was during those weeks that we'd have back-to-back-to-back freezer meals because they require little thought and little time and little energy to get onto the table.

Freezer meals and "dump dinners" play such an important role in a busy mom's kitchen. They help keep dinner on the table night after night, even when life is busy, fast, hectic and chaotic. It's such a blessing having freezer meals "on backup" for the nights each week when you need them.

They also help you stay "one step ahead" with both the prepping and the cooking. This helps keep me balanced in my mental energy, eliminating the 'what's for dinner' question, plus it helps keep me on schedule with getting dinner on the table. It's so much easier for me to punch busy in the face when I have dinner "on demand" in the freezer.

Again, the idea and goal of "dump dinners" is to prep make-ahead meals and keep them in your freezer, to reheat or cook them quickly at a later time. My preferred method is to double 5 recipes, which gets me 10 meals into the freezer in one session. We have built the MyFreezEasy recipes, web app and mobile apps to reflect this philosophy and strategy.

Because it really is the easiest and best way to do "fast food at home."

Before we get to the recipes, I thought I'd share some other freezer cooking hacks with you.

Other General Freezer Cooking Hacks

MyFreezEasy's freezer cooking meal plans are the perfect solution for the crazy busy home chef who wants to have less stress and less mess when getting dinner on the table.

MyFreezEasy meal plans are designed to help you get 10 meals into your freezer in under one hour, using recipes that can quickly be pulled together into freezer bags or trays. Yes, you can easily put together 10 "dump dinners" in an hour's time.

Even with the fast assembly process and cutting out the dinner hour stress, there are still a number of other essential "HACKS" for putting together MyFreezEasy recipes and meal plans.

1. Let the food cool down completely to reduce risk of freezer burn!

2. Package up and remove as much air possible, if using a plastic baggie. If using a plastic container and freezing liquid, be sure to leave enough headspace at the top, as the liquid will expand as it freezes.

3. "Flat freeze" by pressing the food as flat as possible in the baggie. Then you can stack meals and save space in your freezer. Place a torn piece of wax or parchment paper in between the baggies to prevent them from sticking together and tearing.

4. Thaw completely in the fridge overnight or for up to 2 days if it is 'thick.' If you need the food that day, or within 30 minutes, you can let it soak in a warm bowl of water and it will quickly thaw. The thickness of the baggie or container will determine how long it will take to thaw. When I 'quick-thaw' things, it can take anywhere from 20 minutes to an hour.

Note: If utilizing the quick thaw method, please don't leave raw meat out on the counter in a bowl of warm water. Always let raw meat thaw in the refrigerator to keep it at proper cold temperatures.

5. My recommended "stay in the freezer times" are: up to 6 months for regular fridge freezer, or up to 12 months in deep freezer.

6. Do not (I repeat, do NOT!) shop and prep on the same day. Find a time in your schedule that will allow you to shop the morning/afternoon/evening before, then prep the meals the following day.

7. When meat is on sale at your store, prepare the meals with a plan that will use up all the meat and you'll kill two birds with 1 stone.

- You've saved a ton by stocking up on meat that is on sale.
- You've saved a ton of time and sanity by prepping it all for dinner at once.

8. Use the "Prep Day Shopping List by Recipe" (at the back of this cookbook) when in the checkout lane (or even as you are loading and unloading your cart!) to organize ingredients into specific bags so that when you get home, the ingredients are already grouped together by recipe. The bagger might look

at you like you've lost your mind, but you'll be smiling when you get home when it's already organized for your prep & assembly!

9. Drop produce and meats into the fridge in their bags so they are easy to pull out the next day when it's prep time. Leave shelf stable ingredients on the counter, ideally organized in their bags, to make prep set up a cinch.

10. Side Dishes: I leave these very much open and flexible to allow your family to decide which veggies and/or starches are best for your preferences. Make the most of sales and deals on produce and bulk rice or pasta to save big on side dishes too.

Alright, shall we get to the recipes and the Dump Dinners freezer cooking meal plans now?!

Dump Dinners Recipe List

- Apple-BBQ Pork Chops
- Asian Orange Pineapple Pork Chops
- Baked Honey Mustard Pork Chops
- Baked Italian Pork Chops
- Baked Peach Orange Pork Chops
- Baked Salsa Pork Chops
- BBQ Chicken Street Tacos
- Best Italian Beef Sandwiches
- Brown Sugar & Balsamic Pork Chops
- Buffalo Chicken Nachos
- Cheesy Ranch Pork Chops
- Chicken Alfredo with Peas & Bacon
- Cranberry-Mustard Pork Chops
- Creamy Honey Mustard Pork Chops
- Ginger Peach Pork Chops
- Instant Pot Balsamic & Brown Sugar Pulled Pork
- Instant Pot Jerk Pulled Pork Sliders
- Instant Pot Shredded Pork Nachos
- Instant Pot Sweet Chili Pork Chops
- Pineapple BBQ Pork Chops
- Skillet Jamaican Pork Chops
- Sloppy Shredded Beef Sandwiches
- Slow Cooker Apricot Chicken
- Slow Cooker Asian Shredded Beef
- Slow Cooker Baja Shredded Chicken Tacos
- Slow Cooker BBQ Meatballs
- Slow Cooker Brown Sugar Chicken
- Slow Cooker Caribbean Pork Sliders
- Slow Cooker Cheesy Garlic Pork Chops
- Slow Cooker Cheesy Salsa Chicken
- Slow Cooker Chicken & Black Bean Taco Salad
- Slow Cooker Chicken Enchilada Soup
- Slow Cooker Chicken Tortilla Soup
- Slow Cooker Chimichurri Beef Roast
- Slow Cooker Cream Cheese Chicken
- Slow Cooker Creamy Tuscan Chicken
- Slow Cooker Cubano Sandwiches
- Slow Cooker Greek Chicken
- Slow Cooker Green Chile Chicken
- Slow Cooker Honey Garlic Chicken
- Slow Cooker Honey Mustard Shredded Chicken Sandwiches
- Slow Cooker Island Chicken
- Slow Cooker Korean Beef
- Slow Cooker Lemon & Dill Salmon
- Slow Cooker Mississippi Beef Roast
- Slow Cooker Mongolian Beef
- Slow Cooker North Carolina Pulled Pork
- Slow Cooker Ole Chicken
- Slow Cooker Peach Orange Pork Chops
- Slow Cooker Pepperoni Chicken
- Slow Cooker Pineapple Chicken
- Slow Cooker Poppyseed Chicken
- Slow Cooker Pulled Pork Ragu
- Slow Cooker Ranch Chicken Tacos
- Slow Cooker Ranchero Chicken
- Slow Cooker Red Wine Beef Roast
- Slow Cooker Santa Fe Chicken
- Slow Cooker Sesame Salmon
- Slow Cooker Shredded Hawaiian Chicken Sandwiches

Apple-BBQ Pork Chops

Yield: 4 servings
Prep Time: 10 minutes
Cook Time: 40 minutes

Ingredients

- 4 boneless pork chops
- Salt and pepper
- 1/2 cup BBQ sauce
- 1/2 cup applesauce
- Side: rice
- Side: salad
- 9x13 disposable foil tray

Cooking Directions

1. Preheat oven to 375 F. Lightly spray a 9x13-inch baking dish with non-stick cooking spray. Place the pork chops into the baking dish and season both sides with salt and pepper.
2. In a small mixing bowl, whisk together the applesauce and BBQ sauce. Pour over the pork chops and bake in the preheated oven for 30 to 40 minutes, or until pork chops reach 145 F. Let rest for 5 minutes before serving or slicing. Cooking time may vary depending on thickness of the pork chops.
3. Cook the rice, as directed.
4. Prepare salad.
5. Serve Apple-BBQ Pork Chops over rice with salad.

Prepare to Freeze Directions

- In a small mixing bowl, whisk together 1/2 cup applesauce and 1/2 cup BBQ sauce.
- To disposable tray, add the following ingredients:
  - 4 boneless pork chops
  - Salt and pepper
  - Prepared sauce, over the pork chops
- Cover with foil or lid, add label and freeze.

Freeze & Thaw Directions

Put tray in the freezer and freeze up to 6 months in fridge freezer or 12 months in a deep freezer. Thaw in the fridge overnight, or a shallow dish of warm water for about 20 minutes, before transferring to the oven and baking as directed.

Asian Orange Pineapple Pork Chops

Yield: 4 servings
Prep Time: 5 minutes
Cook Time: 20 minutes

Ingredients

- 1 Tbsp canola oil
- 4 boneless pork chops
- 8 oz. can pineapple chunks
- 1/2 cup orange marmalade
- 1/4 cup tamari sauce
- 1/2 tsp ground ginger
- Side: rice
- Side: veggies
- 1 gallon-size freezer baggie

Cooking Directions

1. Open the can of pineapple chunks.
2. Cook the rice, as directed.
3. In a large skillet, heat the oil and brown the pork chops on both sides for 5 minutes.
4. In a small mixing bowl, combine the pineapple chunks and their juices, orange marmalade, tamari sauce, and ginger. Stir and then pour sauce over the pork chops in the skillet. Cover and bring to a simmer over medium heat for 5 minutes, or until pork chops are cooked through.
5. Prepare the veggies.
6. Serve Asian Orange Pineapple Pork Chops over rice with veggies.

Prepare to Freeze Directions

- Open 2 cans of pineapple chunks.
- In a small mixing bowl, combine can of pineapple chunks with juice, 1/2 cup orange marmalade, 1/4 cup tamari sauce, and 1/2 tsp ginger.
- Into gallon-size plastic freezer baggie, add the following ingredients:
  - 4 boneless pork chops
  - Salt and pepper
  - Orange sauce
- Remove as much air as you can and seal. Freeze up to 6 months in your fridge freezer or 12 months in a deep freezer.

Freeze & Thaw Directions

Put baggie in the freezer and freeze up to 6 months in fridge freezer or 12 months in a deep freezer. Thaw in the fridge overnight, or a bowl of warm water for about 20 minutes, before transferring the pork chops and sauce to a large skillet and cooking over medium low heat for 10 to 15 minutes, or until pork chops are cooked through.

Baked Honey Mustard Pork Chops

Yield: 4 servings
Prep Time: 10 minutes
Cook Time: 30 minutes

Ingredients

- 4 boneless pork chops
- 1/4 cup yellow mustard
- 1/4 cup honey
- 1 tsp cider vinegar
- Salt and pepper
- Side: frozen French fries
- Side: veggies
- 1 gallon-size freezer baggie

Cooking Directions

1. Preheat oven to 350 F. Lightly grease a 7x11 or 9x13-inch baking dish with non-stick cooking spray.
2. Place the boneless pork chops into prepared baking dish.
3. In a small mixing bowl, whisk together yellow mustard, honey and cider vinegar. Pour over the pork chops and bake in the preheated oven for 25 to 30 minutes, or until pork chops have cooked through. Cooking time will vary depending on thickness of the pork chops.
4. Serve Honey Mustard Pork Chops with side of fries and veggies.

Prepare to Freeze Directions

- Whisk together 1/4 cup honey, 1/4 cup yellow mustard and 1 tsp cider vinegar in a small bowl.
- Into gallon-size plastic freezer baggie, add the following ingredients:
  - 4 boneless pork chops
  - Salt and pepper
  - Prepared Honey-Mustard sauce
- Remove as much air as possible and seal. Add label and freeze.

Freeze & Thaw Directions

Put tray in the freezer and freeze up to 6 months in fridge freezer or 12 months in a deep freezer. Thaw in the fridge overnight, or a warm shallow dish of water for about 20 minutes, before transferring to the oven and baking as directed.

Baked Italian Pork Chops

Yield: 4 servings
Prep Time: 10 minutes
Cook Time: 30 minutes

Ingredients

- 4 boneless pork chops
- Salt and pepper
- 15 oz. can diced tomatoes
- 1 Tbsp Italian seasoning
- 1 tsp minced garlic
- 1 tsp minced onion
- Side: dinner rolls
- Side: salad
- 1 - 9x13 disposable foil tray

Cooking Directions

1. Preheat the oven to 400 F.
2. Place the pork chops into baking dish and sprinkle with salt and pepper.
3. Open and drain the diced tomatoes.
4. In a small mixing bowl, stir together the drained diced tomatoes, Italian seasoning, minced garlic and minced onion. Pour tomato-spice mixture on top of the pork chops.
5. Bake in the preheated oven for 25 to 30 minutes, or until pork chops are cooked through. Cooking time may vary depending on thickness of the chops.
6. Prepare the salad.
7. Warm the dinner rolls.
8. Serve Baked Italian Pork Chops with salad and dinner rolls.

Prepare to Freeze Directions

- Open and drain can of diced tomatoes.
- In a small mixing bowl, stir together the can of drained diced tomatoes, 1 Tbsp Italian seasoning, 1 tsp minced garlic, and 1 tsp minced onion.
- To disposable tray, add the following ingredients:
  - 4 boneless pork chops
  - Salt and pepper
  - Diced tomatoes-spices mixture
- Cover with foil or lid, add label and freeze.

Freeze & Thaw Directions

Put tray in the freezer and freeze up to 6 months in fridge freezer or 12 months in a deep freezer. Thaw in the fridge overnight, or a warm shallow dish of water for about 20 minutes, before transferring to the oven and baking as directed.

Baked Peach Orange Pork Chops

Yield: 4 servings
Prep Time: 5 minutes
Cook Time: 30 minutes

Ingredients

- 4 boneless pork chops
- Salt and pepper
- 1/4 cup peach preserves
- 1/4 cup orange marmalade
- 2 Tbsp Dijon mustard
- 1 tsp soy sauce
- Side: dinner rolls
- Side: salad
- 1 gallon-size freezer baggie

Cooking Directions

1. Preheat oven to 350 F. Lightly grease a 7x11 or 9x13-inch baking dish with non-stick cooking spray.
2. Place the pork chops into prepared baking dish. Season with salt and pepper.
3. In a small mixing bowl, combine the 1/2 cup peach preserves, 1/2 cup orange marmalade, 4 Tbsp Dijon mustard and 2 tsp soy sauce. Place directly on top of the pork chops, and bake in the preheated oven for 30 minutes, or until pork chops have cooked through. Cooking time will vary depending on thickness of the pork chops.
4. Warm the dinner rolls.
5. Prepare the salad.
6. Serve Baked Peach Orange Pork Chops with dinner rolls and salad.

Prepare to Freeze Directions

- In a small mixing bowl, combine the 1/4 cup peach preserves, 1/4 cup orange marmalade, 2 Tbsp Dijon mustard and 1 tsp soy sauce.
- To gallon-size plastic freezer baggie, add the following ingredients:
  - 4 boneless pork chops
  - Peach-orange sauce
- Remove as much air as possible and seal. Add label to baggie and freeze.

Freeze & Thaw Directions

Put baggie in the freezer and freeze up to 6 months in fridge freezer or 12 months in a deep freezer. Thaw in the fridge overnight, or a bowl of warm water for about 20 minutes, before transferring to the baking dish and cooking as directed.

Baked Salsa Pork Chops

Yield: 4 servings
Prep Time: 10 minutes
Cook Time: 30 minutes

Ingredients

- 4 boneless pork chops
- 1 cup red salsa
- 4 oz. can green chilies
- Salt and pepper
- Garnish: avocado slices
- Side: rice
- Side: salad
- 1 gallon-size freezer baggie

Cooking Directions

1. Preheat oven to 350 F. Lightly grease a 7x11 or 9x13-inch baking dish with non-stick cooking spray.
2. Place the boneless pork chops into prepared baking dish.
3. Pour the red salsa and green chilies around the pork chops. Season with salt and pepper.
4. Bake pork chops in the preheated oven for 30 minutes, or until pork chops have cooked through. Cooking time will vary depending on thickness of the pork chops
5. Cook the rice as directed.
6. Prepare salad and slice avocado garnish.
7. Serve Baked Salsa Pork Chops with avocado slices, over rice with veggies.

Prepare to Freeze Directions

- To gallon-size plastic freezer baggie, add the following ingredients:
    - 4 boneless pork chops
    - 1 cup red salsa
    - 4 oz. can green chilies
    - Salt and pepper
- Remove as much air as possible and seal. Add label to baggie and freeze.

Freeze & Thaw Directions

Put baggie in the freezer and freeze up to 6 months in fridge freezer or 12 months in a deep freezer. Thaw in the fridge overnight, or a bowl of warm water for about 20 minutes, before transferring to the baking dish and baking as directed.

BBQ Chicken Street Tacos

Yield: 4 servings
Prep Time: 10 minutes
Cook Time: 8 hours in slow cooker

Ingredients

- 4 small boneless chicken breasts
- 2 cups BBQ sauce
- 15 oz. can black beans
- Red onion to 1 small red onion
- 12 corn tortillas
- Garnish: shredded cheddar cheese
- Garnish: chopped cilantro
- Side: fruit
- 1 gallon-size freezer baggie

Cooking Directions

1. Chop the red onion.
2. Open, drain and rinse the can of black beans.
3. Spray bottom of slow cooker with cooking spray. Add the chicken breasts, black beans, red onions and pour the BBQ sauce over the top. Add about 1/4 to 1/2 cup of water to thin out the sauce.
4. Set the slow cooker on low and cook for 8 hours. Once cooked, shred the chicken into the BBQ sauce. Spoon shredded chicken and sauce into the corn tortillas and top with garnishes.
5. Prepare fruit and garnishes.
6. Serve BBQ Chicken Street Tacos with side of fruit.

Prepare to Freeze Directions

- Chop the red onion.
- Open, drain and rinse 2 cans of black beans.
- To gallon-size plastic freezer baggie, add the following ingredients:
    - 4 small boneless chicken breasts
    - 15 oz. can black beans
    - Chopped red onion
    - 2 cups BBQ sauce
- Remove as much air as possible and seal. Add label to baggie and freeze.

Freeze & Thaw Directions

Put baggie in the freezer and freeze up to 6 months in fridge freezer or 12 months in a deep freezer. Thaw in the fridge overnight, or a bowl of warm water for about 20 minutes, before adding contents of the baggie to the slow cooker with amount of water listed in the recipe. Set on low and cook for 8 hours. Shred the chicken and make tacos as directed.

Best Italian Beef Sandwiches

Yield: 4 servings
Prep Time: 10 minutes
Cook Time: 8 hours in slow cooker

Ingredients

- 2 lb. beef chuck roast
- 1 small white onion
- 11 oz. jar pepperoncini peppers
- 1 Tbsp Italian seasoning
- 1 tsp garlic powder
- Salt and pepper
- 8 hamburger buns
- Side: salad
- Side: chips
- 1 gallon-size freezer baggie

Cooking Directions

1. Slice the white onion into half-moons.
2. Place the beef roast into the base of the slow cooker and season with salt and pepper. Sprinkle pepperoncini (with juices) and the sliced onions around and on top of the beef roast. Sprinkle the Italian seasoning and garlic powder over the top.
3. Set the slow cooker on low and cook for 8 hours. Once finished cooking, shred the beef with 2 forks and mix into the sauce. Season with salt and pepper to taste.
4. Add the shredded beef, onions and pepperoncini to the buns.
5. Prepare salad.
6. Serve Slow Cooker Best Italian Beef Sandwiches with salad and chips.

Prepare to Freeze Directions

- Slice white onion into half-moons.
- To gallon-size plastic freezer baggie, add the following ingredients:
  - 2 lb. beef chuck roast
  - Sliced onions
  - 11 oz. jar pepperoncini peppers
  - 1 Tbsp Italian seasoning
  - 1 tsp garlic powder
- Remove as much air as possible and seal. Add label to baggie and freeze.

Freeze & Thaw Directions

Put baggie in the freezer and freeze up to 6 months in fridge freezer or 12 months in a deep freezer. Thaw in the fridge overnight, or a bowl of warm water for about 20 minutes, before transferring to the slow cooker and cooking on low for 8 hours. Shred the beef, once cooked, and assemble sandwiches as directed.

Brown Sugar & Balsamic Pork Chops

Yield: 4 servings
Prep Time: 10 minutes
Cook Time: 30 minutes

Ingredients

- 4 boneless pork chops
- Salt and pepper
- 2 Tbsp balsamic vinegar
- 4 tsp brown sugar
- Side: mashed potatoes
- Side: veggies
- 1 gallon-size freezer baggie

Cooking Directions

1. Place the pork chops in the bottom of a glass baking dish. Sprinkle some salt and pepper onto both sides of the pork chops. Then drizzle the balsamic vinegar over the top. Add 1 tsp of brown sugar on top of each pork chop and spread into the vinegar. Let marinate in the fridge for at least 30 minutes*.
2. Preheat oven to 350 F, while pork chops marinate.
3. Bake the pork chops in the preheated oven for 25 to 30 minutes, or until cooked through. Cooking time will depend on the thickness of the pork chops.
4. Serve Brown Sugar & Balsamic Pork Chops with preferred potatoes and veggies.

Prepare to Freeze Directions

- To gallon-size plastic freezer baggie, add the following ingredients:
    - 4 boneless pork chops
    - Salt and pepper
    - 2 Tbsp balsamic vinegar
    - 4 tsp brown sugar
- Remove as much air as possible and seal. Add label to baggie and freeze.

Freeze & Thaw Directions

Put baggie in the freezer and freeze up to 6 months in fridge freezer or 12 months in a deep freezer. Thaw in the fridge overnight, or a bowl of warm water for about 20 minutes, before transferring to the baking dish and baking as directed.

Buffalo Chicken Nachos

Yield: 4 servings
Prep Time: 10 minutes*
Cook Time: 8 hours in slow cooker

Ingredients

- 4 small boneless chicken breasts
- 1 packet ranch dressing mix
- 1 cup buffalo wing sauce
- 1 bag tortilla chips
- 2 cups shredded mozzarella cheese
- Garnish: crumbled blue cheese
- Garnish: chopped celery
- Side: fruit
- 1 gallon-size freezer baggie

Cooking Directions

1. Place the chicken breasts in the base of the slow cooker and sprinkle the ranch dressing mix over the top. Pour the buffalo wing sauce over the top.
2. Set on low and cook for 8 hours. Once the chicken is cooked, shred with 2 forks and combine with the sauce.
3. Preheat the oven to 400 F.
4. Assemble the nachos on baking sheet with tortilla chips, shredded buffalo chicken and shredded mozzarella cheese on top. *Bake in the preheated oven for 10-15 minutes, or until cheese has melted.
5. Prepare fruit.
6. Serve Buffalo Chicken Nachos with crumbled blue cheese and chopped celery garnish, and side of fruit.

Prepare to Freeze Directions

- To gallon-size plastic freezer baggie, add the following ingredients:
  - 4 boneless chicken breasts
  - 1 packet Ranch dressing mix
  - 1 cup buffalo wing sauce
- Remove as much air as possible and seal. Add label to baggie and freeze.

Freeze & Thaw Directions

Put baggie in the freezer and freeze up to 6 months in fridge freezer or 12 months in a deep freezer. Thaw in the fridge overnight, or a bowl of warm water for about 20 minutes, before transferring to the slow cooker and cooking on low for 8 hours. Shred the chicken once it is cooked, and then assemble the nachos as directed.

Cheesy Ranch Pork Chops

Yield: 4 servings
Prep Time: 10 minutes
Cook Time: 30 minutes

Ingredients

- 4 boneless pork chops
- Salt and pepper
- 1/2 cup sour cream
- 1 packet ranch dressing mix
- 1 cup shredded mild cheddar cheese
- Side: veggies
- Side: frozen French fries
- 1 - 9x13 disposable foil tray

Cooking Directions

1. Preheat oven to 350 F. Lightly grease an 9x13-inch baking dish or rimmed baking sheet with non-stick cooking spray.
2. Place the pork chops into the baking dish or baking sheet and season with salt and pepper.
3. In a small mixing bowl, combine the sour cream and Ranch dressing mix. Spread evenly onto the pork chops. Top each covered pork with few pinchfuls of shredded cheese.
4. Bake in the preheated oven for 25 to 30 minutes, or until pork chops are cooked through. Cooking time may vary depending on thickness of the chops.
5. Bake French fries, as directed.
6. Prepare veggies.
7. Serve Cheesy Ranch Pork Chops with veggies and French fries.

Prepare to Freeze Directions

- In a small mixing bowl, combine 1/2 cup sour cream with 1 Ranch dressing mix packet.
- To the disposable tray, add the following ingredients:
  - 4 boneless pork chops
  - Salt and pepper
  - Sour cream sauce, divided evenly to the 4 pork chops
  - 1 cup shredded cheese, sprinkled evenly over the 4 pork chops
- Cover with foil or lid. Add label to tray and freeze.

Freeze & Thaw Directions

Put baggie in the freezer and freeze up to 6 months in fridge freezer or 12 months in a deep freezer. Thaw in the fridge overnight, or a larger tray of warm water for about 20 minutes, before transferring to the baking dish and baking as directed.

Chicken Alfredo with Peas & Bacon

Yield: 4 servings
Prep Time: 10 minutes
Cook Time: 20 minutes

Ingredients

- 3 small boneless chicken breasts
- 4 slices bacon
- 18 oz. jar Alfredo sauce
- 10 oz. bag frozen peas
- Side: small shell pasta noodles
- Side: veggies
- 1 gallon-size freezer baggie

Cooking Directions

1. Cook pasta as directed on package.
2. Add the chicken pieces and bacon to a large skillet with tight fitting lid and saute for 8 to 10 minutes, or until cooked through. Once cooked, stir in the alfredo sauce and frozen peas and let simmer for another 10 minutes until peas are warmed through.
3. Toss the cooked pasta with the sauce before serving.
4. Serve Chicken Alfredo with Peas & Bacon, tossed with pasta and side of veggies.

Prepare to Freeze Directions

- Cut 4 slices bacon into ½" pieces.
- Cut 3 boneless, skinless chicken breasts into ½" pieces.
- To gallon-size plastic freezer baggie, add the following ingredients:
    - Chicken pieces
    - 18 oz. jar Alfredo sauce
    - 10 oz. bag frozen peas
    - Bacon pieces
- Remove as much air as possible and seal. Add label to baggie and freeze.

Freeze & Thaw Directions

Put baggie in the freezer and freeze up to 6 months in fridge freezer or 12 months in a deep freezer. Thaw in the fridge overnight, or a bowl of warm water for about 20 minutes. Add the contents of the freezer baggie to the skillet with about ¾ cup warm water to thin out the alfredo sauce. Bring sauce to bubbling over medium high heat and then reduce to low and simmer for 20 minutes or until chicken is cooked through.

Cranberry-Mustard Pork Chops

Yield: 4 servings
Prep Time: 10 minutes
Cook Time: 35 minutes

Ingredients

- 4 boneless pork chops
- Salt and pepper
- 4 dashes cinnamon
- 15 oz. can whole cranberries
- 1/4 cup spicy mustard
- Side: rice
- Side: veggies
- 1 - 9x13 disposable foil tray

Cooking Directions

1. Preheat oven to 375 F. Spray a 9×13 inch glass baking dish with non-stick cooking spray. and cook on low for 8 hours.
2. Place the pork chops into the baking dish and sprinkle with salt and pepper and add a dash of cinnamon on top of each chop.
3. In a small mixing bowl, combine the whole cranberries with the spicy mustard. Pour the sauce over top of the pork chops and bake in the preheated oven for 30 to 35 minutes, or until pork chops are cooked through. Cooking time may vary, depending on thickness of the chop.
4. Serve Cranberry-Mustard Pork Chops with a side of rice and veggies.

Prepare to Freeze Directions

- Whisk together 15 oz. can whole cranberries sauce & 1/4 cup spicy mustard with the cinnamon in a small bowl.
- To the disposable tray, add the following ingredients:
    - 4 boneless pork chops
    - Prepared cranberry-mustard sauce, over the pork chops
- Cover the tray with foil.

Freeze & Thaw Directions

Put tray in the freezer and freeze up to 6 months in fridge freezer or 12 months in a deep freezer. Thaw in the fridge overnight, or a warm shallow dish of water for about 20 minutes, before transferring to the oven and baking as directed.

Creamy Honey Mustard Pork Chops

Yield: 4 servings
Prep Time: 10 minutes
Cook Time: 30 minutes

Ingredients

- 4 boneless pork chops
- 3 Tbsp heavy cream
- 1/4 cup yellow mustard
- 1/4 cup honey
- 1 tsp cider vinegar
- Salt and pepper
- Side: frozen French fries
- Side: veggies
- 1 gallon-size freezer baggie

Cooking Directions

1. Preheat oven to 350 F. Lightly grease a 7x11 or 9x13-inch baking dish with non-stick cooking spray.
2. Place the boneless pork chops into prepared baking dish.
3. In a small mixing bowl, whisk together the heavy cream, yellow mustard, honey and cider vinegar. Pour over the pork chops and bake in the preheated oven for 25 to 30 minutes, or until pork chops have cooked through. Cooking time will vary depending on thickness of the pork chops.
4. Cook French fries as directed.
5. Prepare veggies.
6. Serve Creamy Honey Mustard Pork Chops with side of fries and veggies.

Prepare to Freeze Directions

- Whisk together 3 Tbsp cream, 1/4 cup honey, 1/4 cup yellow mustard and 1 tsp cider vinegar in a small bowl.
- To gallon-size plastic freezer baggie, add the following ingredients:
  - 4 boneless pork chops
  - Salt and pepper
  - Prepared Honey-Mustard sauce
- Remove as much air as you can and seal. Freeze up to 6 months in your fridge freezer or 12 months in a deep freezer.

Freeze & Thaw Directions

Put tray in the freezer and freeze up to 6 months in fridge freezer or 12 months in a deep freezer. Thaw in the fridge overnight, or a warm shallow dish of water for about 20 minutes, before transferring to the oven and baking as directed.

Ginger Peach Pork Chops

Yield: 4 servings
Prep Time: 10 minutes
Cook Time: 35 minutes

Ingredients

- 4 boneless pork chops
- Salt and pepper
- 1 cup peach preserves
- 1 Tbsp sesame oil
- 1 tsp ground ginger
- Side: veggies
- Side: mashed potatoes
- 1 - 9x9-inch disposable tray

Cooking Directions

1. Preheat the oven to 350 F. Lightly spray a 9x9-inch baking dish with non-stick cooking spray.
2. Place the pork chops into the baking dish and season with salt and pepper.
3. In a small bowl, mix together the peach preserves, sesame oil and ground ginger. Evenly divide and coat each pork chops.
4. Bake in the preheated oven for 25 to 35 minutes, or until pork chops reach 145 F. Let rest for 5 minutes before serving or slicing. Cooking time may vary depending on thickness of the pork chops.
5. Prepare veggies.
6. Prepare mashed potatoes.
7. Serve Ginger Peach Pork Chops with veggies and mashed potatoes.

Prepare to Freeze Directions

- In a small bowl, mix together 1 cup peach preserves, 1 Tbsp sesame oil and 1 tsp ground ginger.
- To disposable tray, add the following ingredients:
  - 4 boneless pork chops
  - Salt and pepper
  - Peach preserve mixture, onto each of the pork chops
- Cover with foil or lid, add label and freeze.

Freeze & Thaw Directions

Put tray in the freezer and freeze up to 6 months in fridge freezer or 12 months in a deep freezer. Thaw in the fridge overnight, or a warm shallow dish of water for about 20 minutes, before transferring to the oven and baking as directed.

Instant Pot Balsamic & Brown Sugar Pulled Pork

Yield: 4 servings
Prep Time: 10 minutes
Cook Time: 40 minutes plus pressure build and release time

Ingredients

- 2 lb. pork roast
- 1/2 cup hot water
- Salt and pepper
- 1/4 cup lime juice
- 3 Tbsp Jerk seasoning
- 1 tsp garlic powder
- 1 tsp onion powder
- 1 tsp ground cumin
- 1 tsp brown sugar
- 1 - 8 oz. can sliced pineapple
- 12 - slider buns
- Garnish: sliced green onions
- Side: fruit
- Side: chips
- 1 - gallon-size freezer baggie

Cooking Directions

1. Place the pork roast into the electric pressure cooker insert with the hot water and season with salt and pepper. Pour the lime juice on and around the pork. Season with the Jerk seasoning, garlic powder, onion powder, ground cumin and brown sugar. Place the pineapple slices over the top.
2. Steam valve: Sealing.
3. Cook on: Manual/High for 40 minutes.
4. Release: Natural or Quick.
5. Once finished cooking, shred the pork with 2 forks and mix into the sauce. Strain before adding the pork to the sliders.
6. Assemble sliders by adding the shredded pork and sliced green onion garnish.
7. Prepare fruit.
8. Serve Instant Pot Jerk Pulled Pork Sliders with fruit and chips.

Prepare to Freeze Directions

- Open and drain 2 cans of sliced pineapple.
- To each gallon-size plastic freezer baggie in a round bowl/dish, add the following ingredients:
    - 2 lb. pork roast
    - Salt and pepper
    - 1/4 cup lime juice
    - 3 Tbsp Jerk seasoning
    - 1 tsp garlic powder
    - 1 tsp onion powder
    - 1 tsp ground cumin
    - 1 tsp brown sugar
    - 1 - 8 oz. can sliced pineapple
- Remove as much air as possible and seal. Add label to baggie and freeze.

Freeze & Thaw Directions

Put baggie in the freezer and freeze up to 6 months in fridge freezer or 12 months in a deep freezer. Thaw in the fridge overnight, or a warm bowl of water for about 20 minutes, before adding contents of bag plus water to electric pressure cooker insert. Pressure cook as directed.

Instant Pot Jerk Pulled Pork Sliders

Yield: 4 servings
Prep Time: 10 minutes
Cook Time: 40 minutes plus pressure build and release time

Ingredients

- 2 lb. pork roast
- 1/2 cup hot water
- Salt and pepper
- 1/4 cup brown sugar
- 2 Tbsp minced onion
- 1 tsp garlic powder
- 1/4 cup balsamic vinegar
- Side: fruit
- Side: potato chips
- 1 - gallon-size freezer baggie

Cooking Directions

1. In a small bowl, whisk together the brown sugar, minced onion, garlic powder and balsamic vinegar.
2. Place the pork roast into the electric pressure cooker insert with the hot water. and season with salt and pepper. Pour the sauce on and around the pork.
3. Steam valve: Sealing.
4. Cook on: Manual/High for 40 minutes.
5. Release: Natural or Quick.
6. Once finished cooking, shred the pork with 2 forks and mix into the sauce. Strain before serving.
7. Prepare fruit.
8. Serve Instant Pot Balsamic & Brown Sugar Pulled Pork with chips and fruit.

Prepare to Freeze Directions

- To each gallon-size plastic freezer baggie in a round bowl/dish, add the following ingredients:
    - 2 lb. pork roast
    - Salt and pepper
    - 1/4 cup brown sugar
    - 2 Tbsp minced onion
    - 1 tsp garlic powder
    - 1/4 cup balsamic vinegar
- Remove as much air as possible and seal. Add label to baggie and freeze.

Freeze & Thaw Directions

Put baggie in the freezer and freeze up to 6 months in fridge freezer or 12 months in a deep freezer. Thaw in the fridge overnight, or a warm bowl of water for about 20 minutes, before adding contents of bag plus water to electric pressure cooker insert. Pressure cook as directed.

Instant Pot Shredded Pork Nachos

Yield: 4 servings
Prep Time: 5 minutes
Cook Time: 40 minutes plus pressure build and release time

Ingredients

- 2 lb. pork roast
- 1 cup hot water
- Salt and pepper
- 1 packet taco seasoning
- 1/4 cup lime juice
- 1 bag corn tortilla chips
- 2 cups shredded mozzarella cheese
- Garnish: chopped cilantro
- Side: veggies
- 1 gallon-size freezer baggie

Cooking Directions

1. Place the pork roast into the electric pressure cooker insert with the hot water. Season with salt and pepper. Sprinkle the taco seasoning and lime juice over the top.
2. Steam valve: Sealing.
3. Cook on: Manual/High for 40 minutes.
4. Release: Natural or Quick.
5. Shred the pork roast when it's finished cooking.
6. Assemble nachos with corn tortillas chips, shredded pork and shredded cheese. Top with chopped cilantro garnish. If needed, place in the microwave or oven to melt the cheese.
7. Prepare veggies.
8. Serve Instant Pot Pork Carnitas Nachos with side of veggies.

Prepare to Freeze Directions

- To gallon-size plastic freezer baggie in a round bowl/dish, add the following ingredients:
  - 2 lb. pork roast
  - Salt and pepper
  - 1 packet taco seasoning
  - 1/4 cup lime juice
  - Do NOT add the water to the freezer baggie
- Remove as much air as possible and seal. Add label to baggie and freeze.

Freeze & Thaw Directions

Put baggie in the freezer and freeze up to 6 months in fridge freezer or 12 months in a deep freezer. Thaw in the fridge overnight, or a bowl of warm water for about 20 minutes, before adding contents of bag plus the water to electric pressure cooker insert. Pressure cook as directed.

Instant Pot Sweet Chili Pork Chops

Yield: 4 servings
Prep Time: 5 minutes
Cook Time: 20 minutes plus pressure build and release time

Ingredients

- 4 boneless pork chops
- 1 cup hot water
- Salt and pepper
- 1/4 cup sweet Thai chili sauce
- Side: rice
- Side: veggies
- 1 gallon-size freezer baggie

Cooking Directions

1. Pour the water into the base of the insert. Add a steamer rack and place the pork chops on the rack and season with salt and pepper. Brush the sweet Thai chili sauce onto each pork chop.
2. Steam valve: Sealing.
3. Cook on: Manual/High for 20 minutes.
4. Release: Natural or Quick.
5. Let rest for 5 minutes before serving or slicing. Cooking time may vary depending on thickness of the pork chops.
6. Cook the rice, as directed.
7. Prepare veggies.
8. Serve Instant Pot Sweet Chili Pork Chops with veggies and rice.

Prepare to Freeze Directions

- To gallon-size plastic freezer baggie in a round bowl/dish, add the following ingredients:
  - 4 boneless pork chops
  - Salt and pepper
  - Sweet Thai chili sauce, brushed onto the pork chops
- Remove as much air as possible, add label and freeze.

Freeze & Thaw Directions

Put baggie in the freezer and freeze up to 6 months in fridge freezer or 12 months in a deep freezer. Thaw in the fridge overnight, or a bowl of warm water for about 20 minutes, before transferring to steam rack in the pressure cooker insert, with hot water underneath the steam rack. Pressure cook as directed.

Pineapple BBQ Pork Chops

Yield: 4 servings
Prep Time: 10 minutes
Cook Time: 30 minutes

Ingredients

- 4 boneless pork chops
- Salt and pepper
- 8 oz. can crushed pineapple
- 1 cup BBQ sauce
- 1 tsp hot sauce
- 1 tsp minced garlic
- 1 tsp minced onion
- Side: dinner rolls
- Side: veggies
- 1 gallon-size freezer baggie

Cooking Directions

1. Preheat the oven to 350 F. Lightly spray baking dish with non-stick cooking spray.
2. Open the can of crushed pineapple. Do not drain.
3. In a small bowl, whisk together the crushed pineapple (with juices), BBQ sauce, hot sauce, minced garlic, and minced onion. Pour a thin layer into the base of the baking dish and spread around.
4. Place the pork chops into the saucy baking dish, season with a little salt and pepper, and then pour the remaining pineapple BBQ sauce evenly over the pork chops.
5. Bake in the preheated oven for 25 to 30 minutes, or until pork chops are cooked through. Cooking time will vary depending on thickness of the pork chops. Let rest 5 minutes before slicing and serving.
6. Warm the dinner rolls.
7. Prepare veggies.
8. Serve Pineapple BBQ Pork Chops with dinner rolls and veggies.

Prepare to Freeze Directions

- Open can of crushed pineapple. Do not drain.
- In a small mixing bowl, whisk together can of crushed pineapple, 1 cup BBQ sauce, 1 tsp hot sauce, 1 tsp minced garlic and 1 tsp minced onion.
- To gallon-size plastic freezer baggie, add the following ingredients:
  - 4 boneless pork chops
  - Salt and pepper
  - Pineapple BBQ sauce
- Remove as much air as possible and seal. Add label to baggie and freeze.

Freeze & Thaw Directions

Put baggie in the freezer and freeze up to 6 months in fridge freezer or 12 months in a deep freezer. Thaw in the fridge overnight, or a bowl of warm water for about 20 minutes, before transferring pork chops and sauce to baking dish and baking as directed.

Skillet Jamaican Pork Chops

Yield: 4 servings
Prep Time: 5 minutes
Cook Time: 10 minutes

Ingredients

- 4 boneless pork chops
- Salt and pepper
- 1 Tbsp canola oil
- 8 oz. can crushed pineapple
- 1 Tbsp Jerk seasoning
- 1 Tbsp brown sugar
- Side: rice
- Side: salad
- 1 gallon-size freezer baggie

Cooking Directions

1. Cook the rice, as directed.
2. Open and drain the canned crushed pineapple.
3. Season both sides of the pork chops with salt and pepper.
4. In a large skillet, heat the oil and brown the pork chops for 2 minutes on each side.
5. Mix together the crushed pineapple, Jerk seasoning and brown sugar. Spread on top of and around the pork chops in the skillet and cook for another 4 to 5 minutes, or until cooked through. Add 1/4 cup water, if needed, to keep sauce from browning too much.
6. Prepare the salad.
7. Serve Skillet Jamaican Pork Chops with rice and salad.

Prepare to Freeze Directions

- Open and drain can of crushed pineapple.
- To gallon-size plastic freezer baggie, add the following ingredients:
    - 4 boneless pork chops
    - Salt and pepper
    - 8 oz. can crushed pineapple
    - 1 Tbsp Jerk seasoning
    - 1 Tbsp brown sugar
- Remove as much air as possible and seal. Add label to baggie and freeze.

Freeze & Thaw Directions

Put baggie in the freezer and freeze up to 6 months in fridge freezer or 12 months in a deep freezer. Thaw in the fridge overnight, or a bowl of warm water for about 20 minutes, before transferring to the skillet to cook the pork chops in the sauce over medium low heat for 8 to 10 minutes, or until pork chops are cooked through.

Sloppy Shredded Beef Sandwiches

Yield: 4 servings
Prep Time: 10 minutes
Cook Time: 8 hours in slow cooker

Ingredients

- 2 lb. beef chuck roast
- Salt and pepper
- 1 small white onion
- 15 oz. can diced tomatoes
- 15 oz. can sloppy joe sauce
- 8 hamburger buns
- Side: salad
- Side: fruit
- 1 gallon-size freezer baggie

Cooking Directions

1. Slice the onion into half moons.
2. Open and drain the diced tomatoes. Open the sloppy joe sauce.
3. Place the beef roast into the base of the slow cooker and season with salt and pepper. Sprinkle the sliced onions over the top, then pour the diced tomatoes and sloppy joe sauce over the top.
4. Set the slow cooker on low and cook for 8 hours. Once finished cooking, shred the beef with 2 forks and mix into the sauce. Assemble sandwiches with hamburger buns and meat sauce.
5. Prepare salad and fruit.
6. Serve Sloppy Shredded Beef Sandwiches with salad and fruit.

Prepare to Freeze Directions

- Slice white onion into half moons.
- Open and drain can of diced tomatoes. Open can of sloppy joe sauce.
- To gallon-size plastic freezer baggie, add the following ingredients:
  - 2 lb. beef chuck roast
  - Salt and pepper
  - Sliced onions
  - Drained diced tomatoes
  - Sloppy joe sauce
- Remove as much air as possible and seal. Add label to baggie and freeze.

Freeze & Thaw Directions

Put baggie in the freezer and freeze up to 6 months in fridge freezer or 12 months in a deep freezer. Thaw in the fridge overnight, or a bowl of warm water for about 20 minutes, before transferring to the slow cooker and cooking on low for 8 hours. Shred the beef and assemble sandwiches as directed.

Slow Cooker Apricot Chicken

Yield: 4 servings
Prep Time: 10 minutes
Cook Time: 6 hours on low

Ingredients

- 6 boneless chicken thighs
- 8 oz. jar apricot preserves
- 1/2 cup French salad dressing
- 2 Tbsp minced onion
- 1 tsp garlic powder
- Salt and pepper
- Side: dinner rolls
- Side: veggies
- 1 gallon-size freezer baggie

Cooking Directions

1. Place the chicken thighs into the base of the slow cooker.
2. In a small mixing bowl, combine the apricot preserves, French dressing, minced onion and garlic powder. Pour over top of the chicken in the slow cooker. Season with a little salt and pepper over the top.
3. Set on low and cook for 6 hours. (Note: if you wish to cook on low for 8 hours, add 1/2 cup water or chicken stock to the sauce.)
4. Warm dinner rolls.
5. Prepare veggies.
6. Serve Slow Cooker Apricot Chicken with dinner rolls and veggies.

Prepare to Freeze Directions

- Whisk together jar of apricot preserves with 1/2 cup French dressing, 2 Tbsp minced onion, 1 tsp garlic powder and a few pinches of salt and pepper.
- To gallon-size plastic freezer baggie, add the following ingredients:
  - 6 boneless, skinless chicken thighs
  - Salt and pepper
  - Prepared apricot sauce
- Remove as much air as possible and seal. Add label and freeze.

Freeze & Thaw Directions

Put baggie in the freezer and freeze up to 6 months in fridge freezer or 12 months in a deep freezer. Thaw in the fridge overnight, or a bowl of warm water for about 20 minutes, before transferring to slow cooker and cooking on low for 6 hours.

Slow Cooker Asian Shredded Beef

Yield: 4 servings
Prep Time: 10 minutes
Cook Time: 8 hours in slow cooker

Ingredients

- 2 lb. beef chuck roast
- Salt and pepper
- 1/3 cup hoisin sauce
- 1/3 cup soy sauce
- 2 Tbsp rice vinegar
- 2 Tbsp honey
- 1 Tbsp sesame oil
- 1 tsp ground ginger
- 1 tsp crushed red pepper
- Garnish: sliced green onions
- Side: rice
- Side: veggies
- 1 gallon-size freezer baggie

Cooking Directions

1. Place the beef roast into the base of the slow cooker and season with salt and pepper.
2. In a mixing bowl, whisk together the hoisin sauce, soy sauce, rice vinegar, honey, sesame oil, ginger and crushed red pepper.
3. Pour the sauce over the beef in the slow cooker.
4. Set the slow cooker on low and cook for 8 hours. Once finished cooking, shred the beef with 2 forks and mix into the sauce.
5. Cook the rice, as directed.
6. Prepare the veggies.
7. Serve Slow Cooker Asian Shredded Beef over rice with veggies and green onion garnish.

Prepare to Freeze Directions

- In a mixing bowl, whisk together 1/3 cup hoisin sauce, 1/3 cup soy sauce, 2 Tbsp rice vinegar, 2 Tbsp honey, 1 Tbsp sesame oil, 1 tsp ground ginger and 1 tsp crushed red pepper.
- To gallon-size plastic freezer baggie, add the following ingredients:
  - 2 lb. beef chuck roast
  - Salt and pepper
  - Prepared Asian sauce
- Remove as much air as possible and seal. Add label to baggie and freeze.

Freeze & Thaw Directions

Put baggie in the freezer and freeze up to 6 months in fridge freezer or 12 months in a deep freezer. Thaw in the fridge overnight, or a bowl of warm water for about 20 minutes, before transferring to the slow cooker and cooking on low for 8 hours. Shred the beef before serving.

Slow Cooker Baja Shredded Chicken Tacos

Yield: 4 servings
Prep Time: 10 minutes
Cook Time: 8 hours in slow cooker

Ingredients

- 3 large boneless chicken breasts
- 1/4 cup brown sugar
- 1 Tbsp cumin
- 1/3 cup salsa
- 4 oz. can green chilies
- Salt and pepper
- 8 flour tortillas
- Garnish: pico de gallo
- 1 gallon-size freezer baggie

Cooking Directions

1. Place the chicken breasts into the base of the slow cooker and add the brown sugar, ground cumin, salsa, green chilies, salt and pepper on top of the chicken.
2. Set the slow cooker on low and cook for 8 hours. Once finished cooking, shred the chicken with 2 forks and mix into the sauce.
3. Spoon the shredded chicken into tortillas and make tacos.
4. Prepare the salad.
5. Serve Slow Cooker Baja Shredded Chicken Tacos with side salad.

Prepare to Freeze Directions

- Open the can of green chilies.
- To gallon-size plastic freezer baggie, add the following ingredients:
    - 3 large boneless chicken breasts
    - 1/4 cup brown sugar
    - 1 Tbsp cumin
    - 1/3 cup salsa
    - Can of green chilies
    - Salt and pepper
- Remove as much air as possible and seal. Add label to baggie and freeze.

Freeze & Thaw Directions

Put baggie in the freezer and freeze up to 6 months in fridge freezer or 12 months in a deep freezer. Thaw in the fridge overnight, or a bowl of warm water for about 20 minutes, before transferring to the slow cooker and cooking on low for 8 hours.

Slow Cooker BBQ Meatballs

Yield: 4 servings
Prep Time: 10 minutes
Cook Time: 4 hours in slow cooker

Ingredients

- 1 lb. precooked frozen meatballs
- 1/2 cup beef broth
- 1 small white onion
- 15 oz. can crushed pineapple
- 2 cups BBQ sauce
- 1 Tbsp honey
- 1 tsp minced garlic
- Salt and pepper
- Side: rice
- Side: veggies
- 1 gallon-size freezer baggie

Cooking Directions

1. Chop the onion. Open and drain the can of pineapple.
2. To the slow cooker, add the precooked meatballs and chopped onion. Pour the beef broth around the meatballs.
3. In a large mixing bowl, whisk together the crushed pineapple, BBQ sauce, honey and minced garlic. Pour this sauce over the meatballs and onions. Set slow cooker on low and cook for 4 hours.
4. Prepare rice and veggies.
5. Serve Slow Cooker BBQ Meatballs with rice and veggies.

Prepare to Freeze Directions

- Chop the onion.
- Open and drain the can of pineapple.
- To gallon-size plastic freezer baggie, add the following ingredients:
  - 1 lb. precooked frozen meatballs
  - Chopped onions
  - 15 oz. can crushed pineapple
  - 2 cups BBQ sauce
  - 1 Tbsp honey
  - 1 tsp minced garlic
  - Do NOT add the beef broth before freezing
- Remove as much air as possible and seal. Add label to baggie and freeze.

Freeze & Thaw Directions

Put baggie in the freezer and freeze up to 6 months in fridge freezer or 12 months in a deep freezer. Thaw in the fridge overnight, or a bowl of warm water for about 20 minutes. Add the beef broth into the base of the slow cooker, then add the meatballs and sauce. Set on low and cook for 4 hours.

Slow Cooker Brown Sugar Chicken

Yield: 4 servings
Prep Time: 10 minutes
Cook Time: 8 hours in slow cooker

Ingredients

- 4 small boneless chicken breasts
- 1/3 cup cider vinegar
- 1/2 cup brown sugar
- 3 Tbsp soy sauce
- 2 tsp minced garlic
- Salt and pepper
- 2 Tbsp cornstarch
- Garnish: crushed red pepper
- Side: rice
- Side: veggies
- 1 gallon-size freezer baggie

Cooking Directions

1. In a small bowl, whisk together the cider vinegar, brown sugar, soy sauce and minced garlic.
2. Place the chicken breasts in the base of the slow cooker and season with salt and pepper. Then pour the brown sugar sauce around and on top of the chicken.
3. Set on low and cook for 8 hours. With 30 minutes, left in the cooking cycle, swirl the cornstarch with a few Tbsp of water to make a slurry, and then stir it into the sauce. Cook for 30 more minutes to allow sauce to thicken.
4. Cook the rice as directed.
5. Prepare veggies.
6. Serve Slow Cooker Brown Sugar Chicken with rice and veggies.

Prepare to Freeze Directions

- In a small bowl, whisk together 1/3 cup cider vinegar, 1/2 cup brown sugar, 3 Tbsp soy sauce and 2 tsp minced garlic.
- To gallon-size plastic freezer baggie, add the following ingredients:
  - 4 boneless chicken breasts
  - Prepared brown sugar-soy sauce mixture
  - Do NOT add the cornstarch before freezing
- Remove as much air as possible and seal. Add label to baggie and freeze.

Freeze & Thaw Directions

Put baggie in the freezer and freeze up to 6 months in fridge freezer or 12 months in a deep freezer. Thaw in the fridge overnight, or a bowl of warm water for about 20 minutes, before transferring to the slow cooker and cooking on low for 8 hours. Thicken with cornstarch at the end of the cooking cycle, as directed.

Slow Cooker Caribbean Pork Sliders

Yield: 4 servings
Prep Time: 10 minutes
Cook Time: 8 hours in slow cooker

Ingredients

- 2 lb. pork roast
- Salt and pepper
- 1 Tbsp minced onion
- 1 tsp garlic powder
- 1 tsp ground cumin
- 1 tsp chipotle chili powder
- 1 cup BBQ sauce
- 16 slider buns
- Garnish: coleslaw
- Side: fruit
- 1 gallon-size freezer baggie

Cooking Directions

1. Place the pork roast into the base of the slow cooker. Season with salt and pepper, the minced onion, garlic powder, ground cumin and chipotle chili powder. Add the BBQ sauce over top. Pour 1 cup hot water around the pork into the base of the slow cooker.
2. Set on low and cook for 8 hours. Once cooked, shred with 2 forks and place the shredded pork onto slider buns with coleslaw.
3. Prepare fruit.
4. Serve Caribbean Pork Sliders with fruit.

Prepare to Freeze Directions

- To gallon-size plastic freezer baggie, add the following ingredients:
  - 2 lb. pork roast
  - Salt and pepper
  - 1 Tbsp minced onion
  - 1 tsp garlic powder
  - 1 tsp ground cumin
  - 1 tsp chipotle chili powder
  - 1 cup BBQ sauce
- Remove as much air as possible and seal. Add label to baggie and freeze.

Freeze & Thaw Directions

Put baggie in the freezer and freeze up to 6 months in fridge freezer or 12 months in a deep freezer. Thaw in the fridge overnight, or a bowl of warm water for about 20 minutes, before transferring to slow cooker. Add 1 cup of hot water and slow cook on low for 8 hours.

Slow Cooker Cheesy Garlic Pork Chops

Yield: 4 servings
Prep Time: 5 minutes
Cook Time: 4 hours in slow cooker

Ingredients

- 4 boneless pork chops
- Salt and pepper
- 2 Tbsp melted butter
- 2 tsp minced garlic
- 1 tsp onion powder
- 1 cup shredded mild cheddar cheese
- Side: dinner rolls
- Side: veggies
- 1 gallon-size freezer baggie

Cooking Directions

1. Place the pork chops into the slow cooker insert and season with salt and pepper.
2. In a small bowl, stir the melted butter, minced garlic, and onion powder. Brush it onto the pork chops. Add a few pinchfuls of shredded mild cheddar cheese onto each pork chop.
3. Slow cook on low for 4 hours. Let rest for 5 minutes before serving or slicing.
4. Prepare veggies.
5. Warm the dinner rolls.
6. Serve Slow Cooker Cheesy Garlic Pork Chops with veggies and dinner rolls.

Prepare to Freeze Directions

- In a small bowl, stir 2 Tbsp melted butter, 2 tsp minced garlic, and 1 tsp onion powder.
- To each gallon size freezer baggie, add the following ingredients:
  - 4 boneless pork chops
  - Melted butter mixture, brushed onto each pork chop
- Remove as much air as possible, add label and freeze.

Freeze & Thaw Directions

Put bag in the freezer and freeze up to 6 months in fridge freezer or 12 months in a deep freezer. Thaw in the fridge overnight, or a shallow dish of warm water for about 20 minutes, before transferring to the slow cooker, adding shredded cheese onto pork chops and cooking as directed. If cooking from frozen, add 1/2 cup of water and cook on low for 8 hours.

Slow Cooker Cheesy Salsa Chicken

Yield: 4 servings
Prep Time: 10 minutes
Cook Time: 8 hours in slow cooker

Ingredients

- 4 small boneless chicken breasts
- 1 cup red salsa
- 1 packet taco seasoning
- 1/2 cup sour cream
- 2 cups shredded cheese
- Salt and pepper
- Side: rice
- Side: salad
- 1 gallon-size freezer baggie

Cooking Directions

1. Place the chicken breasts in the base of the slow cooker and pour the red salsa and taco seasoning over and around the chicken. (Note: Do not add the sour cream before slow cooking.)
2. Set on low and cook for 8 hours. With 30 minutes, left in the cooking cycle, stir in the sour cream and let finish cooking. Once finished cooking, add the shredded cheese on top and let melt. Season with salt and pepper to taste.
3. Cook the rice as directed.
4. Prepare the salad.
5. Serve Slow Cooker Cheesy Salsa Chicken with shredded cheese garnish over rice with salad.

Prepare to Freeze Directions

- To gallon-size plastic freezer baggie, add the following ingredients:
    - 4 boneless chicken breasts
    - 1 cup red salsa
    - 1 packet taco seasoning
    - Do NOT add the sour cream or shredded cheese before freezing.
- Remove as much air as possible and seal. Add label to baggie and freeze.

Freeze & Thaw Directions

Put baggie in the freezer and freeze up to 6 months in fridge freezer or 12 months in a deep freezer. Thaw in the fridge overnight, or a bowl of warm water for about 20 minutes, before transferring to the slow cooker and cooking on low for 8 hours. Stir in the sour cream at the end of the cooking cycle as directed. Top with shredded cheese, once finished cooking.

Slow Cooker Chicken & Black Bean Taco Salad

Yield: 4 servings
Prep Time: 10 minutes
Cook Time: 8 hours in slow cooker

Ingredients

- 4 small boneless chicken breasts
- 15 oz. can black beans
- 1 cup red salsa
- 1 packet taco seasoning
- 1 Salt and pepper
- Garnish: guacamole
- Side: shredded lettuce
- Side: veggies
- 1 gallon-size freezer baggie

Cooking Directions

1. Open, drain and rinse the black beans.
2. Place the chicken breasts in the base of the slow cooker and pour the black beans, salsa, and taco seasoning over the top.
3. Set on low and cook for 8 hours. Once finished cooking, shred the chicken into the sauce. Season with salt and pepper to taste.
4. Prepare the salad with lettuce, shredded chicken and black beans and guacamole topping.
5. Prepare veggies.
6. Serve Slow Cooker Chicken & Black Bean Taco Salad with guacamole and veggies.

Prepare to Freeze Directions

- Open, drain and rinse can of black beans.
- To gallon-size plastic freezer baggie, add the following ingredients:
    - 4 small boneless chicken breasts
    - Can of black beans
    - 1 cup red salsa
    - 1 packet taco seasoning
    - Salt and pepper
- Remove as much air as possible and seal. Add label to baggie and freeze.

Freeze & Thaw Directions

Put baggie in the freezer and freeze up to 6 months in fridge freezer or 12 months in a deep freezer. Thaw in the fridge overnight, or a bowl of warm water for about 20 minutes, before transferring to the slow cooker and cooking on low for 8 hours. Shred the chicken and assemble salad as directed.

Slow Cooker Chicken Enchilada Soup

Yield: 4 servings
Prep Time: 10 minutes
Cook Time: 8 hours in slow cooker

Ingredients

- 3 boneless chicken breasts
- 15 oz. can pinto beans
- 15 oz. can black beans
- 15 oz. diced tom & green chile
- 15 oz. can diced tomato with green chilies
- 1 packet taco seasoning
- 1 Tbsp chili powder
- 2 cups chicken stock
- Salt and pepper
- Garnish: shredded Monterrey Jack cheese
- Side: veggies
- 1 gallon-size freezer baggie

Cooking Directions

1. Open the pinto beans, black beans, diced tomatoes with green chilies and tomato paste.
2. Place the chicken breasts, pinto beans, black beans, diced tomatoes with green chilies and tomato paste into the base of the slow cooker. Sprinkle in the taco seasoning and chili powder, then pour in the chicken stock plus 4 cups hot water.
3. Set the slow cooker on low and cook for 8 hours. Once finished cooking, shred the chicken with 2 forks and mix into the soup. Season with salt and pepper to taste. Add a garnish of shredded Monterrey Jack cheese to each bowl.
4. Prepare veggies.
5. Serve Slow Cooker Chicken Enchilada Soup with veggies.

Prepare to Freeze Directions

- Open 1 can of pinto beans, 1 can of black beans, 1 can of diced tomatoes with green chilies, and 1 can of tomato paste.
- To gallon-size plastic freezer baggie, add the following ingredients:
    - 3 boneless chicken breasts
    - Can of pinto beans
    - Can of black beans
    - Can of diced tomatoes with green chilies
    - Can of tomato paste
    - 1 packet taco seasoning
    - 1 Tbsp chili powder
    - 2 cups chicken stock
    - Salt and pepper
- Remove as much air as possible and seal. Add label to baggie and freeze.

Freeze & Thaw Directions

Put baggie in the freezer and freeze up to 6 months in fridge freezer or 12 months in a deep freezer. Thaw in the fridge overnight, or a bowl of warm water for about 20 minutes, before transferring to the slow cooker with 4 cups hot water and cooking on low for 8 hours.

Slow Cooker Chicken Tortilla Soup

Yield:	4 servings
Prep Time:	10 minutes
Cook Time:	8 hours in slow cooker

Ingredients

- 3 large boneless chicken breasts
- 1 red bell pepper
- 15 oz. can tomato sauce
- 15 oz. can corn
- 2 Tbsp taco seasoning
- 2 cups chicken stock
- 8 corn tortillas
- Garnish: shredded cheese
- 1 gallon-size freezer baggie

Cooking Directions

1. Seed and dice the red bell pepper.
2. To the slow cooker, add the chicken, tomato sauce, taco seasoning, canned corn, red bell pepper, and chicken stock. Set slow cooker on low and cook for 8 hours.
3. Before serving, use 2 forks to pull the chicken apart in the soup. Then ladle soup into bowls and add the tortilla strips into each bowl and let them soak up some of the liquid. Top with shredded cheese, if preferred.
4. Optional: If you wish to thicken the soup, add 1/2 to 1 tsp cornstarch or 2 Tbsp masa harina.
5. Serve Slow Cooker Chicken Tortilla Soup with tortilla strip topping.

Prepare to Freeze Directions

- Open the can of corn.
- Seed and dice the red bell pepper.
- Open the can of tomato sauce.
- To gallon-size plastic freezer baggie, add the following ingredients:
    - 3 boneless, skinless chicken breasts
    - Diced red bell pepper
    - Can of corn
    - Can of tomato sauce
    - 2 Tbsp taco seasoning
    - 2 cups chicken stock
    - Do NOT add the tortillas to the freezer meal bag
- Remove as much air as possible and seal. Add label to baggie and freeze.

Freeze & Thaw Directions

Put baggie in the freezer and freeze up to 6 months in fridge freezer or 12 months in a deep freezer. Thaw in the fridge overnight, or a bowl of warm water for about 20 minutes, before transferring to the slow cooker and cooking on low for 8 hours. Ladle into bowls and add tortilla strips and shredded cheese garnish.

Slow Cooker Chimichurri Beef Roast

Yield:	4 servings
Prep Time:	10 minutes
Cook Time:	8 hours in slow cooker

Ingredients

- 2 lbs beef chuck roast
- 7 oz. jar chimichurri sauce
- Salt and pepper
- Side: black beans
- Side: rice
- Side: veggies
- 1 gallon-size freezer baggie

Cooking Directions

1. Place the beef roast into the base of the slow cooker and season with salt and pepper. Spread the chimichurri sauce directly over the roast. Note: if you slow cooker "runs hot" and overcooks meat, you might want to add a cup of water or beef broth.
2. Set the slow cooker on low and cook for 8 hours.
3. Cook the rice as directed.
4. Prepare the veggies and black beans.
5. Serve Slow Cooker Chimichurri Beef Roast with rice and beans and side of veggies.

Prepare to Freeze Directions

- To gallon-size plastic freezer baggie, add the following ingredients:
  - 2 lb beef chuck roast
  - Salt and pepper
  - 1 jar of chimichurri sauce
- Remove as much air as possible and seal. Add label to baggie and freeze.

Freeze & Thaw Directions

Put baggie in the freezer and freeze up to 6 months in fridge freezer or 12 months in a deep freezer. Thaw in the fridge overnight, or a bowl of warm water for about 20 minutes, before transferring to the slow cooker and cooking on low for 8 hours.

Slow Cooker Cream Cheese Chicken

Yield: 4 servings
Prep Time: 10 minutes
Cook Time: 8 hours in slow cooker

Ingredients

- 4 small boneless chicken breasts
- Salt and pepper
- 10 oz. can cream of mushroom
- 1/2 cup chicken stock
- 1 packet ranch dressing mix
- 1 tsp minced garlic
- 8 oz. cream cheese
- Side: egg noodles
- Side: salad
- 1 gallon-size freezer baggie

Cooking Directions

1. Place the chicken into the slow cooker insert. Season with salt and pepper.
2. In a small mixing bowl, whisk together the cream of mushroom soup, chicken stock, Ranch dressing mix and minced garlic. Pour over the chicken. Do NOT add the cream cheese at the start of slow cooking.
3. Set the slow cooker on low and cook for 8 hours. With 30 minutes left in the cooking cycle, stir in the cream cheese. Stir it well, then close the lid and let the slow cooking cycle finish.
4. Cook the egg noodles, as directed.
5. Prepare the salad.
6. Serve Slow Cooker Cream Cheese Chicken over noodles with side salad.

Prepare to Freeze Directions

- In a small mixing bowl, whisk together the can of cream of mushroom soup, 1 cup chicken stock, 1 packet Ranch dressing mix and 1 tsp minced garlic.
- To gallon-size plastic freezer baggie, add the following ingredients:
    - 4 small boneless chicken breasts
    - Salt and pepper
    - Prepared sauce
    - Do NOT add the cream cheese to freezer bag
- Remove as much air as possible and seal. Add label to baggie and freeze.

Freeze & Thaw Directions

Put baggie in the freezer and freeze up to 6 months in fridge freezer or 12 months in a deep freezer. Thaw in the fridge overnight, or a bowl of warm water for about 20 minutes, before transferring to the slow cooker and cooking on low for 8 hours. With 30 minutes left in cooking cycle, shred the chicken and stir in the cream cheese as directed.

Slow Cooker Creamy Tuscan Chicken

Yield:	4 servings
Prep Time:	15 minutes
Cook Time:	8 hours in slow cooker

Ingredients

- 4 small boneless chicken breasts
- 24 oz. jar Alfredo sauce
- 7 oz. jar sun-dried tomatoes
- 10 oz. box frozen spinach
- 1 tsp minced garlic
- Salt and pepper
- Garnish: grated Parmesan cheese
- Side: pasta
- Side: salad
- 1 gallon-size freezer baggie

Cooking Directions

1. Thaw and drain the spinach. Slice the sun-dried tomatoes into strips, if needed.
2. In a large mixing bowl, combine the alfredo sauce, sun-dried tomatoes, spinach and minced garlic. Mix well.
3. Place the chicken breasts in the base of the slow cooker and season with salt and pepper. Then pour the alfredo sauce mixture over the chicken. Set on low and cook for 8 hours.
4. Cook the pasta, as directed.
5. Prepare the salad.
6. Serve Slow Cooker Creamy Tuscan Chicken over pasta with side salad.

Prepare to Freeze Directions

- Thaw and drain the box of spinach. Slice 1 jar of sun-dried tomatoes into strips, if needed.
- In a large mixing bowl, combine 1 jar of alfredo sauce with the sun-dried tomatoes strips and drained spinach with 1 tsp minced garlic. Mix well.
- To gallon-size plastic freezer baggie, add the following ingredients:
  - 4 boneless chicken breasts
  - Prepared alfredo-sun dried tomato combo
- Remove as much air as possible and seal. Add label to baggie and freeze.

Freeze & Thaw Directions

Put baggie in the freezer and freeze up to 6 months in fridge freezer or 12 months in a deep freezer. Thaw in the fridge overnight, or a bowl of warm water for about 20 minutes, before transferring to the slow cooker and cooking on low for 8 hours.

Slow Cooker Cubano Sandwiches

Yield: 4 servings
Prep Time: 5 minutes
Cook Time: 8 hours in slow cooker

Ingredients

- 2 lbs. pork roast
- Salt and pepper
- 1 cup orange juice
- 1 tsp ground cumin
- 4 hoagie rolls
- 8 sandwich pickles
- 1 Tbsp mayonnaise
- 1 Tbsp Dijon mustard
- 8 slices ham deli meat
- 4 slices Swiss cheese
- Side: fruit
- 1 gallon-size freezer baggie

Cooking Directions

1. Place the pork roast into the base of the slow cooker and season with salt and pepper. Pour the orange juice on and around the pork and season with the ground cumin.
2. Set the slow cooker on low and cook for 8 hours. Once finished cooking, shred the pork with 2 forks and mix into the sauce. Strain before adding the pork to the sandwiches.
3. Assemble sandwiches by adding the shredded pork, ham, Swiss cheese with mayo and mustard onto the hoagie buns with pickles. Warm in oven or press in panini press.
4. Prepare fruit.
5. Serve Slow Cooker Cubano Sandwiches with fruit.

Prepare to Freeze Directions

- To gallon-size plastic freezer baggie, add the following ingredients:
- To gallon-size plastic freezer baggie, add the following ingredients:
    - 2 lb. pork roast
    - Salt and pepper
    - 1 cup orange juice
    - 1 tsp ground cumin
- Remove as much air as possible and seal. Add label to baggie and freeze.

Freeze & Thaw Directions

Put baggie in the freezer and freeze up to 6 months in fridge freezer or 12 months in a deep freezer. Thaw in the fridge overnight, or a bowl of warm water for about 20 minutes, before transferring to the slow cooker and cooking on low for 8 hours. Assemble Cubano Sandwiches as directed.

Slow Cooker Greek Chicken

Yield: 4 servings
Prep Time: 10 minutes
Cook Time: 8 hours in slow cooker

Ingredients

- 4 small boneless chicken breasts
- 1 cup green olives
- 2 Tbsp olive oil
- 2 Tbsp lemon juice
- 1 tsp minced garlic
- 1 tsp dried oregano
- 1/2 tsp pepper
- Garnish: feta cheese crumbles
- Side: rice
- Side: salad
- 1 gallon-size freezer baggie

Cooking Directions

1. Chop the green olives.
2. In a small bowl, whisk together the chopped olives, olive oil, lemon juice, minced garlic, dried oregano and pepper.
3. Place the chicken breasts in the base of the slow cooker and pour the olive sauce over the top.
4. Set on low and cook for 8 hours.
5. Cook the rice as directed.
6. Prepare salad.
7. Serve Slow Cooker Greek Chicken with crumbled feta cheese garnish, over rice with salad.

Prepare to Freeze Directions

- Chop 1 cup of green olives.
- In a small bowl, whisk together the chopped olives, 2 Tbsp olive oil, 2 Tbsp lemon juice, 1 tsp minced garlic, 1 tsp dried oregano, and 1/2 tsp pepper.
- To gallon-size plastic freezer baggie, add the following ingredients:
  - 4 boneless chicken breasts
  - Olive sauce
- Remove as much air as you can and seal. Freeze up to 6 months in your fridge freezer or 12 months in a deep freezer.

Freeze & Thaw Directions

Put baggie in the freezer and freeze up to 6 months in fridge freezer or 12 months in a deep freezer. Thaw in the fridge overnight, or a bowl of warm water for about 20 minutes, before transferring to the slow cooker and cooking on low for 8 hours.

Slow Cooker Green Chile Chicken

Yield: 4 servings
Prep Time: 10 minutes
Cook Time: 8 hours in slow cooker

Ingredients

- 8 boneless chicken thighs
- 1/4 cup lime juice
- 2 tsp ground cumin
- 1 tsp garlic powder
- 4 tomatillos
- 1/2 small white onion
- 4 oz. can green chilies
- Salt and pepper
- Garnish: lime wedges and cilantro
- Side: rice
- Side: veggies
- 1 gallon-size freezer baggie

Cooking Directions

1. Peel off the husk and cut the tomatillos into quarters. Dice white onion.
2. Place the chicken thighs into the base of the slow cooker and add the lime juice, ground cumin, garlic powder, quartered tomatillos, diced onion and green chilies on top of the chicken. Season with salt and pepper.
3. Set the slow cooker on low and cook for 8 hours.
4. Cook the rice, as directed.
5. Once finished cooking, shred the chicken with 2 forks and mix into the sauce. Spoon the shredded chicken over the rice.
6. Prepare veggies and garnish.
7. Serve Slow Cooker Green Chile Chicken over rice, garnished with lime wedges and cilantro with a side of veggies.

Prepare to Freeze Directions

- Peel off the husk and cut tomatillos into quarters.
- Dice the onion.
- Open the can of green chilies.
- To gallon-size plastic freezer baggie, add the following ingredients:
    - 8 boneless chicken thighs
    - 1/4 cup lime juice
    - 2 tsp ground cumin
    - 1 tsp garlic powder
    - Quartered tomatillos
    - Diced onions
    - Can of green chilies
    - Salt and pepper
- Remove as much air as possible and seal. Add label to baggie and freeze.

Freeze & Thaw Directions

Put baggie in the freezer and freeze up to 6 months in fridge freezer or 12 months in a deep freezer. Thaw in the fridge overnight, or a bowl of warm water for about 20 minutes, before transferring to the slow cooker and cooking on low for 8 hours.

Slow Cooker Honey Garlic Chicken

Yield: 4 servings
Prep Time: 10 minutes
Cook Time: 8 hours in slow cooker

Ingredients

- 4 small boneless chicken breasts
- 1/2 cup soy sauce
- 1/2 cup honey
- 1/4 cup teriyaki sauce
- 2 Tbsp rice vinegar
- 1 tsp sesame oil
- 2 tsp minced garlic
- 1 tsp minced onion
- 1 tsp ground ginger
- 2 Tbsp cornstarch
- Garnish: sliced green onions
- Side: rice
- Side: salad
- 1 gallon-size freezer baggie

Cooking Directions

1. Place the chicken into the slow cooker insert. Season with salt and pepper.
2. In a small mixing bowl, whisk together the soy sauce, honey, teriyaki sauce, rice vinegar, sesame oil, minced garlic, minced onion, and ground ginger. Do NOT add the cornstarch at the start of slow cooking.
3. Set the slow cooker on low and cook for 8 hours. With 30 minutes left in the cooking cycle, shred the chicken with 2 forks. Then mix the cornstarch with the same amount of water and swirl into the sauce in the slow cooker. Stir it well, then close the lid and let the slow cooking cycle finish.
4. Cook the rice, as directed.
5. Prepare the salad.
6. Serve Slow Cooker Honey Garlic Chicken over rice with side salad.

Prepare to Freeze Directions

- In a small mixing bowl, whisk together 1/2 cup soy sauce, 1/2 cup honey, 1/4 cup teriyaki sauce, 42 Tbsp rice vinegar, 1 tsp sesame oil, 1 tsp minced garlic, 1 tsp minced onion, and 1 tsp ground ginger.
- To gallon-size plastic freezer baggie, add the following ingredients:
  - 4 small boneless chicken breasts
  - Salt and pepper
  - Prepared marinade
  - Do NOT add the cornstarch to freezer bag
- Remove as much air as possible and seal. Add label to baggie and freeze.

Freeze & Thaw Directions

Put baggie in the freezer and freeze up to 6 months in fridge freezer or 12 months in a deep freezer. Thaw in the fridge overnight, or a bowl of warm water for about 20 minutes, before transferring to the slow cooker and cooking on low for 8 hours. With 30 minutes left in cooking cycle, shred the chicken and swirl in the cornstarch as directed.

Slow Cooker Honey Mustard Shredded Chicken Sandwiches

Yield: 4 servings
Prep Time: 10 minutes
Cook Time: 8 hours in slow cooker

Ingredients

- 2 large boneless chicken breasts
- 1/4 cup honey
- 3 Tbsp Dijon mustard
- 1 tsp vinegar
- 4 sliced Provolone cheese
- 4 sandwich buns
- Side: veggies
- 1 gallon-size freezer baggie

Cooking Directions

1. Place the chicken breasts in the base of the slow cooker. Whisk together honey, Dijon mustard and vinegar in a small bowl and pour over chicken breasts.
2. Set the slow cooker on low and cook for 8 hours.
3. Note: if your slow cooker "runs hot" and has dried out meat in the past, you might want to add 1/2 to 1 cup of water or chicken stock to keep the inside of the slow cooker humid and prevent the meat from drying out.
4. Once cooked, use 2 forks to shred the chicken before serving on sandwich buns with slice of cheese.
5. Serve Slow Cooker Honey Mustard Shredded Chicken Sandwiches with veggies.

Prepare to Freeze Directions

- Whisk together 1/4 cup honey, 3 Tbsp Dijon mustard and 1 tsp vinegar.
- To gallon-size plastic freezer baggie, add the following ingredients:
    - 2 large boneless, skinless chicken breasts
    - Salt and pepper
    - Prepared marinade
- Remove as much air as possible and seal. Add label to baggie and freeze.

Freeze & Thaw Directions

Put baggie in the freezer and freeze up to 6 months in fridge freezer or 12 months in a deep freezer. Thaw in the fridge overnight, or a bowl of warm water for about 20 minutes, before transferring to the slow cooker and cooking on low for 8 hours.

Slow Cooker Island Chicken

Yield:	4 servings
Prep Time:	10 minutes
Cook Time:	8 hours in slow cooker

Ingredients

- 4 small boneless chicken breasts
- Salt and pepper
- 1 cup orange juice
- 1/2 cup lime juice
- 1/4 cup brown sugar
- 1 Tbsp cumin
- 1 tsp paprika
- 20 oz. can pineapple slices
- Side: rice
- Side: veggies
- 1 gallon-size freezer baggie

Cooking Directions

1. Place the chicken breasts into the base of slow cooker and season with salt and pepper.
2. In a large mixing bowl, whisk together the orange juice, lime juice, brown sugar, ground cumin, and paprika.
3. Pour the marinade over the chicken, then add the pineapple slices around and on top of the chicken and marinade. Slow cook on low for 8 hours.
4. Cook the rice as directed.
5. Prepare the veggies.
6. Serve Slow Cooker Island Chicken over rice with veggies.

Prepare to Freeze Directions

- Open and drain the can of pineapple.
- To gallon-size plastic freezer baggie, add the following ingredients:
    - 4 small boneless chicken breasts
    - Salt and pepper
    - 1 cup orange juice
    - 1/2 cup lime juice
    - 1/4 cup brown sugar
    - 1 Tbsp cumin
    - 1 tsp paprika
    - Pineapple slices
- Remove as much air as you can and seal. Freeze up to 6 months in your fridge freezer or 12 months in a deep freezer.

Freeze & Thaw Directions

Put baggie in the freezer and freeze up to 6 months in fridge freezer or 12 months in a deep freezer. Thaw in the fridge overnight, or a bowl of warm water for about 20 minutes, before transferring to the slow cooker and cooking on low for 8 hours.

Slow Cooker Korean Beef

Yield: 4 servings
Prep Time: 10 minutes
Cook Time: 8 hours in slow cooker

Ingredients

- 2 lb. stew beef
- 1 cup beef stock
- 1/4 cup soy sauce
- 3 Tbsp sesame oil
- 1 Tbsp minced onion
- 1 tsp garlic powder
- 1 tsp ground ginger
- Salt and pepper
- 1 tsp cornstarch
- Garnish: sliced green onions
- Side: rice
- Side: salad
- 1 gallon-size freezer baggie

Cooking Directions

1. Place the stew beef pieces into the base of the slow cooker.
2. In a small bowl, whisk together the beef stock, soy sauce, sesame oil, minced onion, garlic powder, ground ginger and salt and pepper. Pour over the beef in the slow cooker and set on low. Cook for 8 hours.
3. With 30 minutes left in the cooking cycle, stir the 1 tsp cornstarch with 3 Tbsp water in a small bowl, then swirl it into the sauce in the slow cooker and finish cooking. It will thicken as it finishes cooking.
4. Cook the rice, as directed.
5. Prepare the salad.
6. Serve Slow Cooker Korean Beef with green onion garnish over rice with salad.

Prepare to Freeze Directions

- In a small bowl, whisk together 1 cups beef stock, 1/4 cup soy sauce, 3 Tbsp sesame oil, 1 tsp minced onion, 1 tsp garlic powder, 1 tsp ground ginger and salt and pepper.
- To gallon-size plastic freezer baggie, add the following ingredients:
    - 2 lb. stew beef
    - Prepared sauce
    - Do NOT add cornstarch to the freezer meal baggie
- Remove as much air as possible and seal. Add label to baggie and freeze.

Freeze & Thaw Directions

Put baggie in the freezer and freeze up to 6 months in fridge freezer or 12 months in a deep freezer. Thaw in the fridge overnight, or a bowl of warm water for about 20 minutes, before transferring to the slow cooker and cooking on low for 8 hours. Stir in cornstarch as directed, with 30 minutes left in cooking cycle.

Slow Cooker Lemon & Dill Salmon

Yield: 4 servings
Prep Time: 10 minutes
Cook Time: 1 to 1 ½ hours on high

Ingredients

- 1 lb. salmon fillet
- Salt and pepper
- 2 tsp lemon juice
- 2 tsp fresh dill
- Side: veggies
- Side: rice
- 1 gallon-size freezer baggie

Cooking Directions

1. Place a large piece of parchment paper into the base of the slow cooker. The parchment paper is to make it easier to lift the salmon out of the slow cooker after it cooks.
2. Cut the salmon fillets into 4 individual portions.
3. Place the 4 salmon fillets flat on the parchment paper, skin side down. Sprinkle each with little salt and pepper over the top. Drizzle lemon juice over the salmon pieces. Place fresh chopped dill sprigs on salmon.
4. Set on high and cook for 1 to 1 ½ hours.
5. Cook rice as directed on package.
6. Prepare veggies, as needed.
7. Once salmon is cooked, carefully lift it out of the slow cooker onto a shallow serving dish. Remove skin and serve.
8. Serve Lemon & Dill Salmon with rice and veggies.

Prepare to Freeze Directions

- Cut 1 lb. salmon into 4 - 1/4 lb. fillets.
- Halve 2 lemons.
- Finely chop 2 tsp fresh dill.
- To gallon-size plastic freezer baggie, add the following ingredients:
  - Salmon fillets
  - Salt and pepper
  - Juice from 2 lemons
  - Chopped dill
- Remove as much air as possible and seal. Add label to baggie and freeze.

Freeze & Thaw Directions

Put baggie in the freezer and freeze up to 6 months in fridge freezer or 12 months in a deep freezer. Thaw in the fridge overnight, or a bowl of warm water for about 20 minutes, before transferring to the slow cooker lined with parchment paper, and cooking on high for 1 to 1 ½ hours.

Slow Cooker Mississippi Beef Roast

Yield: 4 servings
Prep Time: 10 minutes
Cook Time: 8 hours in slow cooker

Ingredients

- 2 lb. beef chuck roast
- 1 packet ranch dressing mix
- 8 pepperoncini peppers
- 1 tsp pepper
- Side: dinner rolls
- Side: veggies
- 1 gallon-size freezer baggie

Cooking Directions

1. Place the beef roast in the base of the slow cooker and season with Ranch dressing mix. Add the pepperoncini peppers directly on the roast and sprinkle the pepper on top. Set slow cooker on low and cook for 8 hours.
2. Warm the dinner rolls.
3. Prepare veggies.
4. Serve Slow Cooker Mississippi Mud Beef Roast with veggies and dinner rolls.

Prepare to Freeze Directions

- To gallon-size plastic freezer baggie, add the following ingredients:
    - 2 lb. beef chuck roast
    - 1 packet Ranch dressing mix
    - 8 pepperoncini peppers
    - 1 tsp pepper
- Remove as much air as possible and seal. Add label to baggie and freeze.

Freeze & Thaw Directions

Put baggie in the freezer and freeze up to 6 months in fridge freezer or 12 months in a deep freezer. Thaw in the fridge overnight, or a bowl of warm water for about 20 minutes, before transferring to the slow cooker and cooking on low for 8 hours.

Slow Cooker Mongolian Beef

Yield: 4 servings
Prep Time: 10 minutes
Cook Time: 4 hours in slow cooker

Ingredients

- 1 1/2 lb. beef for stirfry
- 2 Tbsp canola oil
- 2 Tbsp cornstarch
- 2 garlic cloves
- 1 Tbsp minced onion
- 1 tsp minced ginger
- 2/3 cup soy sauce
- 2/3 cup water
- 2/3 cup brown sugar
- 1/2 lb. bag shredded matchstick carrots
- 1 tsp crushed red pepper
- Garnish: green onion
- Side: rice
- Side: veggies
- 1 gallon-size freezer baggie

Cooking Directions

1. In a small mixing bowl toss the beef with the oil and cornstarch. Place into the base of the slow cooker.
2. In a mixing bowl, whisk together the crushed garlic, minced onion, minced ginger, soy sauce, water and brown sugar. Pour over the beef in the slow cooker. Add the shredded carrots and crushed red pepper over the top.
3. Set on low and cook for 4 hours. If you need to cook it on low for 8 hours, add an extra ½ cup of water.
4. Cook the rice, as directed.
5. Prepare veggies.
6. Serve Slow Cooker Mongolian Beef over rice with veggies and optional green onion garnish.

Prepare to Freeze Directions

- Toss together 1 1/2 lb. beef strips with 2 Tbsp canola oil and 2 Tbsp cornstarch.
- Whisk together 2 crushed garlic cloves, 1 Tbsp minced onion, 1 tsp minced ginger, 2/3 cup soy sauce, 2/3 cup water, 2/3 cup brown sugar.
- To gallon-size plastic freezer baggie, add the following ingredients:
  - Beef strips coated in cornstarch
  - Prepared sauce
  - 1/2 lb. bag shredded matchstick carrots
  - 1 tsp crushed red pepper
- Remove as much air as possible and seal. Add label to baggie and freeze.

Freeze & Thaw Directions

Put baggie in the freezer and freeze up to 6 months in fridge freezer or 12 months in a deep freezer. Thaw in a bowl of warm water for about 20 minutes, before transferring to the slow cooker and cooking on low for 4 hours.

Slow Cooker North Carolina Pulled Pork

Yield: 4 servings
Prep Time: 5 minutes
Cook Time: 8 hours in slow cooker

Ingredients

- 2 lb. pork roast
- Salt and pepper
- 2 cups BBQ sauce
- 1 tsp vinegar
- 1 tsp garlic powder
- 1 tsp onion powder
- 1 small bag Coleslaw mix
- 4 hamburger buns
- Side: fruit
- Side: chips
- 1 gallon-size freezer baggie

Cooking Directions

1. Place the pork roast into the base of the slow cooker and season with salt and pepper. Pour the BBQ sauce and vinegar on and around the pork and season with the garlic powder and onion powder.
2. Set the slow cooker on low and cook for 8 hours. Once finished cooking, shred the pork with 2 forks and mix into the BBQ sauce. Strain before adding the pork to the sandwiches.
3. Prepare the Coleslaw mix as directed.
4. Assemble sandwiches by adding the shredded pork and Coleslaw to the hamburger buns.
5. Prepare fruit.
6. Serve Slow Cooker North Carolina Pulled Pork Sandwiches with fruit and chips.

Prepare to Freeze Directions

- To gallon-size plastic freezer baggie, add the following ingredients:
    - 2 lb. pork roast
    - Salt and pepper
    - 2 cups BBQ sauce
    - 1 tsp vinegar
    - 1 tsp garlic powder
    - 1 tsp onion powder
- Remove as much air as possible and seal. Add label to baggie and freeze.

Freeze & Thaw Directions

Put baggie in the freezer and freeze up to 6 months in fridge freezer or 12 months in a deep freezer. Thaw in the fridge overnight, or a bowl of warm water for about 20 minutes, before transferring to the slow cooker and cooking on low for 8 hours. Assemble North Carolina Pulled Pork Sandwiches as directed.

Slow Cooker Ole Chicken

Yield: 4 servings
Prep Time: 10 minutes
Cook Time: 8 hours in slow cooker

Ingredients

- 4 small boneless chicken breasts
- 10 oz. can cream of mushroom
- 10 oz. can cream of chicken
- 1 cup sour cream
- 2 Tbsp minced onion
- 1 tsp minced garlic
- 1 cup salsa
- 8 flour tortillas
- 1 cup shredded Pepper jack cheese
- Side: rice
- Side: beans
- 1 gallon-size freezer baggie

Cooking Directions

1. Slice the chicken into thin strips.
2. In a large mixing bowl, stir together the cream of mushroom soup, cream of chicken soup, sour cream, minced onion and minced garlic.
3. To the base of the slow cooker, add 1 layer of tortillas, then the half of the soup mixture, then half of the chicken strips, then salsa, then repeat layers of tortilla, soup mixture, chicken and salsa. Add final layer of tortillas on top.
4. Set on low and cook for 8 hours. With 15 minutes, add the shredded cheese on top and let cheese melt. Cut out slices of the cheesy chicken and serve.
5. Cook the rice as directed.
6. Prepare the beans, as directed.
7. Serve Slow Cooker Ole Chicken with rice and beans.

Prepare to Freeze Directions

- Open the can of cream of mushroom soup and the can of cream of chicken soup. Whisk together in small bowl with the sour cream, minced onion and minced garlic.
- Thinly slice 4 small boneless chicken breasts.
- To gallon-size plastic freezer baggie, add the following ingredients:
  - Mushroom-chicken soup mixture
  - Sliced chicken
  - Do not add salsa, tortillas or cheese.
- Remove as much air as possible and seal. Add label to baggie and freeze.

Freeze & Thaw Directions

Put baggie in the freezer and freeze up to 6 months in fridge freezer or 12 months in a deep freezer. Thaw in the fridge overnight, or a bowl of warm water for about 20 minutes, before layering the tortillas, soup-chicken mixture and salsa into the slow cooker as directed. Set on low and cook for 8 hours.

Slow Cooker Peach Orange Pork Chops

Yield: 4 servings
Prep Time: 5 minutes
Cook Time: 4 hours in slow cooker

Ingredients

- 4 boneless pork chops
- Salt and pepper
- 1/4 cup peach preserves
- 1/4 cup orange marmalade
- 2 Tbsp Dijon mustard
- 1 tsp soy sauce
- Side: dinner rolls
- Side: salad
- 1 gallon-size freezer baggie

Cooking Directions

1. Place the pork chops into the base of the slow cooker with 1 cup of water in the base/insert. Season with salt and pepper.
2. In a small mixing bowl, combine the 1/2 cup peach preserves, 1/2 cup orange marmalade, 4 Tbsp Dijon mustard and 2 tsp soy sauce. Place directly on top of the pork chops.
3. Set the slow cooker on low and cook for 4 hours.
4. Warm the dinner rolls.
5. Prepare the salad.
6. Serve Slow Cooker Peach Orange Pork Chops with dinner rolls and salad.

Prepare to Freeze Directions

- In a small mixing bowl, combine the 1/4 cup peach preserves, 1/4 cup orange marmalade, 2 Tbsp Dijon mustard and 1 tsp soy sauce.
- To gallon-size plastic freezer baggie, add the following ingredients:
  - 4 boneless pork chops
  - Peach-orange sauce
- Remove as much air as possible and seal. Add label to baggie and freeze.

Freeze & Thaw Directions

Put baggie in the freezer and freeze up to 6 months in fridge freezer or 12 months in a deep freezer. Thaw in the fridge overnight, or a bowl of warm water for about 20 minutes, before transferring to the slow cooker and cooking on low for 4 hours.

Slow Cooker Pepperoni Chicken

Yield: 4 servings
Prep Time: 10 minutes
Cook Time: 6 hours in slow cooker

Ingredients

- 4 small boneless chicken breasts
- 1 1/2 cups pizza sauce
- 20 pepperonis
- 1 cup shredded mozzarella cheese
- Salt and pepper
- Garnish: grated Parmesan cheese
- Side: pasta
- Side: veggies
- 1 gallon-size freezer baggie

Cooking Directions

1. Place the chicken breasts in the base of the slow cooker and pour the pizza sauce directly over the chicken. Add the pepperonis around and on top of the chicken.
2. Set on low and cook for 6 hours. With 30 minutes remaining in the cooking cycle, add the shredded mozzarella cheese right onto each piece of chicken and let finish cooking. Use a slotted spoon to remove the chicken and drain the juices from the slow cooker. Garnish with grated Parmesan cheese.
3. Cook the pasta as directed.
4. Prepare veggies.
5. Serve Slow Cooker Pepperoni Chicken over pasta rice with veggies.

Prepare to Freeze Directions

- To gallon-size plastic freezer baggie, add the following ingredients:
  - 4 boneless chicken breasts
  - 1 1/2 cups pizza sauce
  - 20 pepperonis
- Remove as much air as possible and seal. Add label to baggie and freeze.

Freeze & Thaw Directions

Put baggie in the freezer and freeze up to 6 months in fridge freezer or 12 months in a deep freezer. Thaw in the fridge overnight, or a bowl of warm water for about 20 minutes, before transferring to the slow cooker and cooking on low for 6 hours. Strain and add cheese and garnish at the end of the cooking cycle.

Slow Cooker Pineapple Chicken

Yield: 4 servings
Prep Time: 10 minutes
Cook Time: 8 hours in slow cooker

Ingredients

- 4 small boneless chicken breasts
- 3/4 cup chicken stock
- 1/4 cup brown sugar
- 3 Tbsp soy sauce
- 1 tsp minced garlic
- 20 oz. can pineapple chunks
- Salt and pepper
- 1 Tbsp cornstarch
- Garnish: sesame seeds
- Side: rice
- Side: veggies
- 1 gallon-size freezer baggie

Cooking Directions

1. Drain the pineapple juice into a small bowl. Set the drained can of pineapple to the side. Add the chicken stock, brown sugar, soy sauce and minced garlic to the bowl with the pineapple juice.
2. Place the chicken breasts in the base of the slow cooker and pour the pineapple chunks around the chicken. Season with salt and pepper. Pour the pineapple-soy sauce mixture over the top.
3. Set on low and cook for 8 hours. With 30 minutes, left in the cooking cycle, swirl the cornstarch with a few Tbsp of water and stir it into the sauce. Cook for 30 more minutes to allow sauce to thicken.
4. Cook the rice as directed.
5. Prepare veggies.
6. Serve Slow Cooker Pineapple Chicken with sesame seed garnish over rice with veggies.

Prepare to Freeze Directions

- Drain and reserve the pineapple juice from 1 can of pineapple chunks in small bowl. To the pineapple juice, add 3/4 cup chicken stock, 1/4 cup brown sugar, 3 Tbsp soy sauce and 1 tsp minced garlic.
- To gallon-size plastic freezer baggie, add the following ingredients:
  - 4 boneless chicken breasts
  - Drained pineapple chunks
  - Prepared sauce
  - Do NOT add the cornstarch before freezing
- Remove as much air as possible and seal. Add label to baggie and freeze.

Freeze & Thaw Directions

Put baggie in the freezer and freeze up to 6 months in fridge freezer or 12 months in a deep freezer. Thaw in the fridge overnight, or a bowl of warm water for about 20 minutes, before transferring to the slow cooker and cooking on low for 8 hours. Thicken with cornstarch at the end of the cooking cycle as directed.

Slow Cooker Poppyseed Chicken

Yield: 4 servings
Prep Time: 10 minutes
Cook Time: 8 hours in slow cooker

Ingredients

- 4 boneless chicken breasts
- 10 oz. can cream of mushroom
- 1 cup sour cream
- 2 cups shredded cheddar cheese
- 2 cups crushed Ritz crackers
- 1 tsp poppyseed
- 4 Tbsp melted butter
- Side: rice
- Side: salad
- 1 gallon-size freezer baggie

Cooking Directions

1. Place the chicken breasts into the insert of the slow cooker. Season with salt and pepper.
2. In a small mixing bowl, combine the cream of mushroom soup (undiluted) and the sour cream. Pour over top of the chicken and then top with the shredded cheese.
3. In a small mixing bowl, toss together the crushed crackers, poppyseeds and butter. Place on top of the shredded cheese.
4. Set the slow cooker on low and cook for 8 hours, or until chicken is cooked through. Cooking time may vary depending on thickness of the chicken.
5. Cook the rice, as directed.
6. Prepare the salad.
7. Serve Slow Cooker Poppyseed Chicken with rice and salad.

Prepare to Freeze Directions

- Open the can of cream of mushroom soup. Do not dilute with milk.
- Melt 4 Tbsp butter.
- In a small mixing bowl, combine the cream of mushroom soup with 1 cup of sour cream.
- In a small mixing bowl, toss together 2 cups of crushed crackers, 1 tsp poppyseed and 4 Tbsp melted butter.
- To each gallon size freezer baggie, add the following ingredients in this order:
  - 4 boneless chicken breasts
  - Cream of mushroom soup combo
  - 2 cups shredded cheddar cheese
  - Crushed crackers combo
- Remove as much air as possible and seal. Add label to baggie and freeze.

Freeze & Thaw Directions

Put baggie in the freezer and freeze up to 6 months in fridge freezer or 12 months in a deep freezer. Thaw in the fridge overnight, or a bowl of warm water for about 20 minutes, before transferring to the slow cooker and cooking as directed.

Slow Cooker Pulled Pork Ragu

Yield: 4 servings
Prep Time: 10 minutes
Cook Time: 8 hours in slow cooker

Ingredients

- 2 lb. pork tenderloin
- Salt and pepper
- 28 oz. can crushed tomatoes
- 7 oz. jar roasted red peppers
- 3 tsp minced garlic
- 2 Tbsp Italian seasoning
- Side: pasta
- Side: salad
- 1 gallon-size freezer baggie

Cooking Directions

1. Open the can of crushed tomatoes. Drain the jar of roasted red peppers.
2. Place the pork tenderloin into the base of the slow cooker and season with salt and pepper. Pour the crushed tomatoes, drained roasted red peppers, minced garlic and Italian seasoning over the pork tenderloin.
3. Set the slow cooker on low and cook for 8 hours. Once finished cooking, shred the pork with 2 forks and mix into the ragu sauce.
4. Cook the pasta as directed.
5. Prepare the salad.
6. Serve Slow Cooker Pulled Pork Ragu over pasta with salad.

Prepare to Freeze Directions

- Open the can of crushed tomatoes.
- Open and drain the jar of roasted red peppers.
- To gallon-size plastic freezer baggie, add the following ingredients:
    - 2 lb. pork tenderloin
    - Salt and pepper
    - 28 oz. can crushed tomatoes
    - 7 oz. jar roasted red peppers
    - 3 tsp minced garlic
    - 2 Tbsp Italian seasoning
- Remove as much air as possible and seal. Add label to baggie and freeze.

Freeze & Thaw Directions

Put baggie in the freezer and freeze up to 6 months in fridge freezer or 12 months in a deep freezer. Thaw in the fridge overnight, or a bowl of warm water for about 20 minutes, before transferring to the slow cooker and cooking on low for 8 hours.

Slow Cooker Ranch Chicken Tacos

Yield: 4 servings
Prep Time: 10 minutes
Cook Time: 8 hours in slow cooker

Ingredients

- 4 small boneless chicken breasts
- 1/2 cup chicken stock
- 1 packet ranch dressing mix
- 1 packet taco seasoning
- Salt and pepper
- 8 flour tortillas
- Garnish: coleslaw
- Garnish: Ranch salad dressing
- Side: salad
- 1 gallon-size freezer baggie

Cooking Directions

1. Place the chicken breasts in the base of the slow cooker. Season with salt and pepper.
2. In a small mixing bowl, whisk the chicken stock and Ranch dressing mix together and pour over the chicken. Sprinkle the taco seasoning on top.
3. Set on low and cook for 8 hours. Once cooked, strain off excess liquid and shred the chicken into the sauce. Season with salt and pepper as needed. Assemble tacos with shredded chicken, coleslaw and Ranch dressing into tortillas.
4. Prepare the salad.
5. Serve Slow Cooker Ranch Chicken Tacos with coleslaw garnish and side salad.

Prepare to Freeze Directions

- To gallon-size plastic freezer baggie, add the following ingredients:
  - 4 boneless chicken breasts
  - 1/2 cup chicken stock
  - 1 packet Ranch dressing mix
  - 1 packet taco seasoning
  - Salt and pepper
- Remove as much air as possible and seal. Add label to baggie and freeze.

Freeze & Thaw Directions

Put baggie in the freezer and freeze up to 6 months in fridge freezer or 12 months in a deep freezer. Thaw in the fridge overnight, or a bowl of warm water for about 20 minutes, before transferring to the slow cooker and cooking on low for 8 hours. Strain the liquid, shred the chicken and assemble the tacos, as directed.

Slow Cooker Ranchero Chicken

Yield: 4 servings
Prep Time: 10 minutes
Cook Time: 8 hours in slow cooker

Ingredients

- 2 large boneless chicken breasts
- 4 boneless, skinless chicken thighs
- 15 oz. can diced tomatoes
- 6 oz. can tomato paste
- 1 packet taco seasoning
- Salt and pepper
- Side: rice
- Side: veggies
- 1 gallon-size freezer baggie

Cooking Directions

1. Place the chicken breasts and thighs into the slow cooker insert.
2. In a small bowl, whisk together the diced tomatoes with their juices, the tomato paste and the taco seasoning. Pour the sauce over the top of the chicken.
3. Set the slow cooker on low and cook for 8 hours.
4. Once cooked, pull apart the chicken with 2 forks.
5. Cook rice, as directed.
6. Prepare veggies.
7. Serve Ranchero Chicken over rice with side of veggies.

Prepare to Freeze Directions

- Open the can of diced tomatoes.
- Open the can of tomato paste.
- To gallon-size plastic freezer baggie, add the following ingredients:
  - 2 boneless chicken breasts
  - 4 boneless chicken thighs
  - Can of diced tomatoes
  - Can of tomato paste
  - 1 packet taco seasoning
- Remove as much air as possible and seal. Add label to baggie and freeze.

Freeze & Thaw Directions

Put baggie in the freezer and freeze up to 6 months in fridge freezer or 12 months in a deep freezer. Thaw in the fridge overnight, or a bowl of warm water for about 20 minutes, before transferring to the slow cooker and cooking on low for 8 hours. Shred the chicken and mix with the sauce and use as simple meal, or for enchiladas or burritos or tacos or tostadas.

Slow Cooker Red Wine Beef Roast

Yield: 4 servings
Prep Time: 10 minutes
Cook Time: 8 hours in slow cooker

Ingredients

- 3 lb. beef chuck roast
- Salt and pepper
- 1/4 cup red wine
- 2 tsp minced garlic
- 2 tsp chopped chives
- 3 lb. bag baby potatoes
- 1 cup beef broth
- Side: salad
- 1 gallon-size freezer baggie

Cooking Directions

1. Place the beef chuck roast into the base of the slow cooker and season with salt and pepper. Pour the red wine, minced garlic and chopped chives over the beef roast. Nestle the baby potatoes around the beef roast and then pour in 1 cup beef broth.
2. Set the slow cooker on low and cook for 8 hours.
3. Prepare the salad.
4. Serve Slow Cooker Red Wine Beef Roast and potatoes with side salad.

Prepare to Freeze Directions

- To gallon-size plastic freezer baggie, add the following ingredients:
    - 3 lb. beef roast
    - Salt and pepper
    - 1/4 cup red wine
    - 2 tsp minced garlic
    - 2 tsp chopped chives
    - 3 lbs baby potatoes
    - 1 cup beef broth
- Remove as much air as possible and seal. Add label to baggie and freeze.

Freeze & Thaw Directions

Put baggie in the freezer and freeze up to 6 months in fridge freezer or 12 months in a deep freezer. Thaw in the fridge overnight, or a bowl of warm water for about 20 minutes, before transferring to the slow cooker and cooking on low for 8 hours.

Slow Cooker Santa Fe Chicken

Yield: 4 servings
Prep Time: 10 minutes
Cook Time: 8 hours in slow cooker

Ingredients

- 4 small boneless chicken breasts
- 15 oz. can black beans
- 15 oz. can corn
- 1 cup red salsa
- 1 tsp garlic powder
- 1 tsp ground cumin
- Salt and pepper
- 4 oz. cream cheese
- 8 flour tortillas
- Garnish: cilantro
- Side: veggies
- 1 gallon-size freezer baggie

Cooking Directions

1. Open, drain and rinse the black beans.
2. Open and drain the corn.
3. Place the chicken breasts in the base of the slow cooker and pour the black beans, corn, salsa, garlic powder and ground cumin over the top.
4. Set on low and cook for 8 hours. With 30 minutes, left in the cooking cycle, shred the chicken with forks and stir the cream cheese into the sauce. Cook for 30 more minutes to allow sauce to thicken. Stir again before serving. Season with salt and pepper to taste.
5. Prepare veggies.
6. Serve Slow Cooker Santa Fe Chicken in tortillas with cilantro garnish and side of veggies.

Prepare to Freeze Directions

- Open and drain the can of corn.
- Open, drain and rinse the can of black beans.
- To gallon-size plastic freezer baggie, add the following ingredients:
  - 4 boneless chicken breasts
  - Can of black beans
  - Can of corn
  - 1 cup red salsa
  - 1 tsp garlic powder
  - 1 tsp ground cumin
  - Do NOT add the cream cheese before freezing.
- Remove as much air as possible and seal. Add label to baggie and freeze.

Freeze & Thaw Directions

Put baggie in the freezer and freeze up to 6 months in fridge freezer or 12 months in a deep freezer. Thaw in the fridge overnight, or a bowl of warm water for about 20 minutes, before transferring to the slow cooker and cooking on low for 8 hours. Stir in the cream cheese and shred the chicken with 30 minutes left in the cooking cycle.

Slow Cooker Sesame Salmon

Yield: 4 servings
Prep Time: 10 minutes
Cook Time: 1 to 1 1/2 hours in slow cooker

Ingredients

- 1 lb. salmon fillet
- 3 Tbsp honey
- 2 Tbsp soy sauce
- 1 Tbsp sesame oil
- 1 tsp minced garlic
- 1 tsp ground ginger
- 1/2 tsp cayenne pepper
- Garnish: sesame seeds and green onions
- Side: rice
- Side: veggies
- 1 gallon-size freezer baggie
- 1 piece of parchment paper

Cooking Directions

1. Cut salmon into 4 individual portions. Place the parchment paper into the base of the slow cooker and add the salmon fillets onto the parchment paper.
2. In a small bowl, whisk together the honey, soy sauce, sesame oil, minced garlic, ground ginger and cayenne pepper. Pour over the salmon, like a glaze.
3. Set the slow cooker on low and cook for 1 to 1 1/2 hours, or until salmon is cooked through. Check after 1 hour and continue slow cooking until finished cooking through. When serving, garnish with sesame seeds and sliced green onions.
4. Cook the rice, as directed.
5. Prepare veggies.
6. Serve Slow Cooker Sesame Salmon with rice and veggies.

Prepare to Freeze Directions

- Cut 1 lb. salmon fillet into 4 individual portions.
- In a small bowl, whisk together 3 Tbsp honey, 2 Tbsp soy sauce, 1 Tbsp sesame oil, 1 tsp minced garlic, 1 tsp ground ginger and 1/2 tsp cayenne pepper.
- To gallon-size plastic freezer baggie, add the following ingredients:
  - 4 salmon fillets
  - Prepared marinade-glaze
- Remove as much air as possible and seal. Add label to baggie and freeze.

Freeze & Thaw Directions

Put baggie in the freezer and freeze up to 6 months in fridge freezer or 12 months in a deep freezer. Thaw in the fridge overnight, or a bowl of warm water for about 20 minutes, before transferring to a parchment lined slow cooker and cooking on low for 1 to 1 1/2 hours.

Slow Cooker Shredded Hawaiian Chicken Sandwiches

Yield: 8 servings
Prep Time: 10 minutes
Cook Time: 8 hours in slow cooker

Ingredients

- 4 small boneless chicken breasts
- Salt and pepper
- 1/2 cup BBQ sauce
- 2 - 8 oz. cans crushed pineapple
- 1 small red onion
- 8 hamburger buns
- Side: chips
- 1 gallon-size freezer baggie

Cooking Directions

1. Finely chop the red onion.
2. Place the chicken breasts into the base of the slow cooker. Sprinkle a little salt and pepper over the top. Drizzle BBQ sauce over the chicken breasts and then pour the pineapple juices around the chicken breasts and the pineapple and red onion on top of the chicken.
3. Set on low and cook for 8 hours. Once cooked, pull out the chicken breasts and the pineapple and add to a bowl, then shred with 2 forks.
4. Prepare fruit, as needed.
5. Serve Shredded Hawaiian Chicken Sandwiches with fruit and chips.

Prepare to Freeze Directions

- Finely chop the small red onion.
- Open 2 cans of crushed pineapple. Do not drain.
- To gallon-size plastic freezer baggie, add the following ingredients:
  - 4 small boneless chicken breasts
  - Salt and pepper
  - 1/2 cup BBQ sauce
  - Both cans of pineapple
  - Finely chopped onion
- Remove as much air as possible and seal. Add label to baggie and freeze.

Freeze & Thaw Directions

Put baggie in the freezer and freeze up to 6 months in fridge freezer or 12 months in a deep freezer. Thaw in the fridge overnight, or a bowl of warm water for about 20 minutes, before transferring to the slow cooker and cooking on low for 8 hours.

Freezer Meal Plan #1 - Recipes, Shopping Lists & Instructions

Baked Mexican Pork Chops

Slow Cooker Baja Shredded Chicken Tacos

Slow Cooker Pepperoni Chicken

Slow Cooker Teriyaki Chicken

Slow Cooker Tomato Basil Tortellini Soup

Note: The following meal plans are written with 5 recipes that double to make a total of 10 meals. The shopping lists and instructions are written to make 2 meals worth of each recipe.

1. Baked Mexican Pork Chops

Yield: 4 servings
Active Time: 10 minutes. Cook Time: 35 minutes

Recipe is written to make a single meal. Assembly Prep Directions & Shopping Lists will both contain directions and ingredients to make 2 meals, based on the number of servings you selected.

** This ingredient is used on the day you cook this meal. It is not added at the time you assemble and prepare your meals for the freezer.

Ingredients for Single Meal

- 4 - boneless pork chops
- 1 - 15 oz. can(s) corn
- 1 - 10 oz diced tom & green chile
- 1 - Tbsp ground cumin
- 1 - tsp garlic powder
- - Salt and pepper
- 1 - cup(s) shredded Pepperjack cheese
- Side: - rice**
- Side: - veggies**
- 1 - 9x13 disposable foil tray(s)

Cooking Directions for Single Meal

1. Preheat the oven to 375 F. Lightly spray a small baking dish with non-stick cooking spray.
2. Open and drain the corn. Open and drain the diced tomatoes with green chilies.
3. In a mixing bowl, toss together the corn, diced tomatoes with green chilies, cumin and garlic powder.
4. Place the pork chops into the base of the prepared baking dish and season with salt and pepper on both sides. Pour the corn-tomato mixture over the top.
5. Bake in the preheated oven for 25 to 35 minutes, or until pork chops are cooked through. Add shredded Pepperjack cheese over the top and let melt, before serving.
6. Cook the rice, as directed.
7. Prepare veggies.
8. Serve Baked Mexican Pork Chops with rice and veggies.

Assembly Prep Directions for 2 Meals

- Open and drain 2 cans of corn. Open and drain 2 cans of diced tomatoes with green chilies.
- In a mixing bowl, toss together the corn and diced tomatoes with green chilies with 2 Tbsp cumin and 2 tsp garlic powder.
- To each disposable tray, add the following ingredients:
  - 4 boneless pork chops
  - Half of the corn-tomatoes mixture over the pork chops
  - Do not add the shredded cheese at the time of freezing
- Cover with foil or lid, add label and freeze.

Freeze & Thaw Instructions: *Put tray in the freezer and freeze up to 6 months in fridge freezer or 12 months in a deep freezer. Thaw in the fridge overnight, or a shallow dish of warm water for about 20 minutes, before transferring to the oven and baking as directed.*

Dairy-Free Modifications: *Recipe is dairy-free when you omit the cheese topping.*

Gluten-Free Modifications: *Recipe is gluten-free when served with gluten-free sides.*

2. Slow Cooker Baja Shredded Chicken Tacos

Yield: 4 servings
Active Time: 10 minutes. Cook Time: 8 hours in slow cooker

Recipe is written to make a single meal. Assembly Prep Directions & Shopping Lists will both contain directions and ingredients to make 2 meals, based on the number of servings you selected.

** This ingredient is used on the day you cook this meal. It is not added at the time you assemble and prepare your meals for the freezer.

Ingredients for Single Meal

- 3 - large boneless chicken breasts
- 1/4 - cup(s) brown sugar
- 1 - Tbsp cumin
- 1/3 - cup(s) salsa
- 1 - 4 oz. can(s) green chiles
- - Salt and pepper
- 8 - flour tortillas**
- Garnish: - pico de gallo**
- 1 - gallon-size freezer baggie(s)

Cooking Directions for Single Meal

1. Place the chicken breasts into the base of the slow cooker and add the brown sugar, ground cumin, salsa, green chilies, salt and pepper on top of the chicken.
2. Set the slow cooker on low and cook for 8 hours. Once finished cooking, shred the chicken with 2 forks and mix into the sauce.
3. Spoon the shredded chicken into tortillas and make tacos.
4. Prepare the salad.
5. Serve Slow Cooker Baja Shredded Chicken Tacos with side salad.

Assembly Prep Directions for 2 Meals

- Open 2 cans of green chiles.
- To each gallon-size plastic freezer baggie, add the following ingredients:
  - 3 large boneless chicken breasts
  - 1/4 cup brown sugar
  - 1 Tbsp cumin
  - 1/3 cup salsa
  - Half of the canned green chiles
  - Salt and pepper
- Remove as much air as possible and seal. Add label to baggie and freeze.

Freeze & Thaw Instructions: *Put baggie in the freezer and freeze up to 6 months in fridge freezer or 12 months in a deep freezer. Thaw in the fridge overnight, or a warm bowl of water for about 20 minutes, before transferring to the slow cooker and cooking on low for 8 hours.*

Dairy-Free Modifications: *Recipe is dairy-free when served with dairy-free sides.*

Gluten-Free Modifications: *Recipe is gluten-free if you use corn tortillas in place of the flour tortillas.*

3. Slow Cooker Pepperoni Chicken

Yield: 4 servings
Active Time: 10 minutes. Cook Time: 6 hours in slow cooker

Recipe is written to make a single meal. Assembly Prep Directions & Shopping Lists will both contain directions and ingredients to make 2 meals, based on the number of servings you selected.

** This ingredient is used on the day you cook this meal. It is not added at the time you assemble and prepare your meals for the freezer.

Ingredients for Single Meal

- 4 - small boneless chicken breasts
- 1 1/2 - cup(s) pizza sauce
- 20 - pepperonis
- 1 - cup(s) shredded mozzarella cheese
- - Salt and pepper
- Garnish: - grated Parmesan cheese**
- Side: - pasta**
- Side: - veggies**
- 1 - gallon-size freezer baggie(s)

Cooking Directions for Single Meal

1. Place the chicken breasts in the base of the slow cooker and pour the pizza sauce directly over the chicken. Add the pepperonis around and on top of the chicken.
2. Set on low and cook for 6 hours. With 30 minutes remaining in the cooking cycle, add the shredded mozzarella cheese right onto each piece of chicken and let finish cooking. Use a slotted spoon to remove the chicken and drain the juices from the slow cooker. Garnish with grated Parmesan cheese.
3. Cook the pasta as directed.
4. Prepare veggies.
5. Serve Slow Cooker Pepperoni Chicken over pasta rice with veggies.

Assembly Prep Directions for 2 Meals

- To each gallon-size plastic freezer baggie, add the following ingredients:
  - 4 boneless chicken breasts
  - 1 1/2 cups pizza sauce
  - 20 pepperonis
- Remove as much air as possible and seal. Add label to baggie and freeze.

Freeze & Thaw Instructions: *Put baggie in the freezer and freeze up to 6 months in fridge freezer or 12 months in a deep freezer. Thaw in the fridge overnight, or a warm bowl of water for about 20 minutes, before transferring to the slow cooker and cooking on low for 8 hours. Thicken with cornstarch at the end of the cooking cycle as directed.*

Special Notes: *Garnish with your favorite pizza toppings like sliced black olives, chopped bell peppers or sliced mushrooms.*

Dairy-Free Modifications: *Unfortunately, there is not a great dairy-free option for this meal.*

Gluten-Free Modifications: *Recipe is gluten-free if served with gluten-free pasta.*

4. Slow Cooker Teriyaki Chicken

Yield: 4 servings
Active Time: 10 minutes. Cook Time: 8 hours in slow cooker

Recipe is written to make a single meal. Assembly Prep Directions & Shopping Lists will both contain directions and ingredients to make 2 meals, based on the number of servings you selected.

** This ingredient is used on the day you cook this meal. It is not added at the time you assemble and prepare your meals for the freezer.

Ingredients for Single Meal

- 3 - large boneless chicken breasts
- - Salt and pepper
- 12 - oz. julienned carrots
- 2 - cup(s) teriyaki sauce
- 1 - Tbsp cornstarch**
- Side: - rice**
- Side: - veggies**
- 1 - gallon-size freezer baggie(s)

Cooking Directions for Single Meal

1. Add 1 cup of water to the base of the slow cooker. Place chicken breasts into the base of the slow cooker and season with salt and pepper. Add the shredded carrots over the top, then pour the teriyaki sauce over the chicken and carrots. Set on low and cook for 8 hours.
2. With 30 minutes left in the cooking cycle, remove the chicken breasts and most of the shredded carrots. Place on plate or bowl to shred or slice. Stir 1 Tbsp of cornstarch in small bowl with 2 tsp water. Stir the water-cornstarch mixture into the sauce in the slow cooker and let the cooking cycle finish and the sauce will thicken.
3. Cook rice, as directed.
4. Prepare veggies.
5. Serve Slow Cooker Teriyaki Chicken over rice with veggies.

Assembly Prep Directions for 2 Meals

- To each gallon-size plastic freezer baggie, add the following ingredients:
  - 3 large boneless, skinless chicken breasts
  - Salt and pepper
  - 12 oz. julienned carrots or "matchstick" carrots
  - 2 cups teriyaki sauce
  - Note: Do NOT add cornstarch to the freezer bag.
- Remove as much as air as possible and seal.

Freeze & Thaw Instructions: *Put baggie in the freezer and freeze up to 6 months in fridge freezer or 12 months in a deep freezer. Thaw in the fridge overnight, or a warm bowl of water for about 20 minutes, before transferring to the slow cooker with 1 cup of water and cooking on low for 8 hours. Thicken sauce after cooking, as directed.*

Special Notes: *You might need to add more cornstarch depending on how much sauce is left in the slow cooker.*

Dairy-Free Modifications: *Recipe is dairy-free when served with dairy-free sides.*

Gluten-Free Modifications: *Use gluten-free teriyaki sauce for gluten-free meal.*

5. Slow Cooker Tomato Basil Tortellini Soup

Yield: 4 servings
Active Time: 10 minutes. Cook Time: 1 hour in slow cooker

Recipe is written to make a single meal. Assembly Prep Directions & Shopping Lists will both contain directions and ingredients to make 2 meals, based on the number of servings you selected.

** This ingredient is used on the day you cook this meal. It is not added at the time you assemble and prepare your meals for the freezer.

Ingredients for Single Meal

- 1 - 26 oz. jar(s) spaghetti sauce
- 20 - oz. box(es) of cheese tortellini
- 8 - oz. box(es) sliced mushrooms
- 6 - oz. bag(s) fresh spinach
- 4 - fresh basil leaves
- 1 - Tbsp minced onion
- 1 - tsp minced garlic
- 4 - cup(s) vegetable stock
- - Salt and pepper
- Garnish: - shredded Parmesan cheese**
- Side: - salad**
- 1 - gallon-size freezer baggie(s)

Cooking Directions for Single Meal

1. Place all the ingredients, except the garnish and sides, into the base of the slow cooker and pour in 2 cups of hot water.
2. Set the slow cooker on low and cook for 1 hour, or until tortellini are tender. Once finished cooking, ladle soup into serving bowls immediately to keep the pasta from overcooking.
3. Prepare the salad.
4. Serve Tomato Basil Tortellini Soup with Parmesan cheese garnish and salad.

Assembly Prep Directions for 2 Meals

- To each gallon-size plastic freezer baggie, add the following ingredients:
    - 1 - 26 oz. jar spaghetti sauce
    - 1 - 20 oz. box cheese tortellini
    - 8 oz. sliced mushrooms
    - 6 oz. fresh spinach
    - 4 fresh basil leaves
    - 1 Tbsp minced onion
    - 1 tsp minced garlic
    - 4 cups vegetable stock
    - Salt and pepper
- Remove as much air as possible and seal. Add label to baggie and freeze.

Freeze & Thaw Instructions: *Put baggie in the freezer and freeze up to 6 months in fridge freezer or 12 months in a deep freezer. Thaw in the fridge overnight, or a warm bowl of water for about 20 minutes, before transferring to the slow cooker and cooking on low for 1 hour.*

Special Notes: *Use chicken stock for non-vegetarian meal. Stovetop cooking directions: thaw and cook over medium low heat for 20 to 30 minutes, or until tortellini is cooked and tender.*

Dairy-Free Modifications: *Unfortunately, there isn't a great dairy-free alternative for this meal.*

Gluten-Free Modifications: *Unfortunately, there isn't a great gluten-free alternative for this meal.*

Complete Shopping List by Recipe

1. Baked Mexican Pork Chops

- ☐ 8 boneless pork chops
- ☐ 2 - 15 oz. can(s) corn
- ☐ 2 - 10 oz. cans diced tomatoes with green chilies
- ☐ 2 Tbsp ground cumin
- ☐ 2 tsp garlic powder
- ☐ Salt and pepper
- ☐ 2 cup(s) shredded Pepperjack cheese
- ☐ **Side:** rice
- ☐ **Side:** veggies
- ☐ 2 - 9x13 disposable foil tray(s)

2. Slow Cooker Baja Shredded Chicken Tacos

- ☐ 6 large boneless chicken breasts
- ☐ 1/2 cup(s) brown sugar
- ☐ 2 Tbsp cumin
- ☐ 2/3 cup(s) salsa
- ☐ 2 - 4 oz. can(s) green chiles
- ☐ Salt and pepper
- ☐ 16 flour tortillas
- ☐ **Garnish:** pico de gallo
- ☐ 2 gallon-size freezer baggie(s)

3. Slow Cooker Pepperoni Chicken

- ☐ 8 small boneless chicken breasts
- ☐ 3 cup(s) pizza sauce
- ☐ 40 pepperonis
- ☐ 2 cup(s) shredded mozzarella cheese
- ☐ Salt and pepper
- ☐ **Garnish:** grated Parmesan cheese
- ☐ **Side:** pasta
- ☐ **Side:** veggies
- ☐ 2 gallon-size freezer baggie(s)

4. Slow Cooker Teriyaki Chicken

- ☐ 6 large boneless chicken breasts
- ☐ Salt and pepper
- ☐ 2 - 12 oz. bags julienned carrots
- ☐ 4 cup(s) teriyaki sauce
- ☐ 2 Tbsp cornstarch
- ☐ **Side:** rice
- ☐ **Side:** veggies
- ☐ 2 gallon-size freezer baggie(s)

5. Slow Cooker Tomato Basil Tortellini Soup

- ☐ 2 - 26 oz. jar(s) spaghetti sauce
- ☐ 2 - 20 oz. box(es) of cheese tortellini
- ☐ 2 - 8 oz. box(es) sliced mushrooms
- ☐ 2 - 6 oz. bag(s) fresh spinach
- ☐ 8 fresh basil leaves
- ☐ 2 Tbsp minced onion
- ☐ 2 tsp minced garlic
- ☐ 8 cup(s) vegetable stock
- ☐ Salt and pepper
- ☐ **Garnish:** shredded Parmesan cheese
- ☐ **Side:** salad
- ☐ 2 gallon-size freezer baggie(s)

Complete Shopping List by Store Section/Category

Meat

- ☐ 8 boneless pork chops
- ☐ 12 large boneless chicken breasts
- ☐ 8 small boneless chicken breasts

Produce

- ☐ **Side:** veggies
- ☐ **Garnish:** pico de gallo
- ☐ 2 - 12 oz. bags julienned carrots
- ☐ 2 - 8 oz. box(es) sliced mushrooms
- ☐ 2 - 6 oz. bag(s) fresh spinach
- ☐ 8 fresh basil leaves
- ☐ **Side:** salad

Pantry Staples - Canned, Boxed

- ☐ 2 - 15 oz. can(s) corn
- ☐ 2 - 10 oz. cans diced tomatoes with green chilies
- ☐ **Side:** rice
- ☐ 2/3 cup(s) salsa
- ☐ 2 - 4 oz. can(s) green chiles
- ☐ 8 cup(s) vegetable stock

Starchy Sides

- ☐ 16 flour tortillas
- ☐ **Side:** pasta

Sauces/Condiments

- ☐ 3 cup(s) pizza sauce
- ☐ 4 cup(s) teriyaki sauce
- ☐ 2 - 26 oz. jar(s) spaghetti sauce

Spices

- ☐ 2 Tbsp ground cumin
- ☐ 2 tsp garlic powder
- ☐ Salt and pepper
- ☐ 1/2 cup(s) brown sugar
- ☐ 2 Tbsp cumin
- ☐ 40 pepperonis
- ☐ 2 Tbsp cornstarch
- ☐ 2 Tbsp minced onion
- ☐ 2 tsp minced garlic

Dairy/Frozen

- ☐ 2 cup(s) shredded Pepperjack cheese
- ☐ 2 cup(s) shredded mozzarella cheese
- ☐ **Garnish:** grated Parmesan cheese
- ☐ 2 - 20 oz. box(es) of cheese tortellini
- ☐ **Garnish:** shredded Parmesan cheese

Supplies

- ☐ **Side:** 2 - 9x13 disposable foil tray(s)
- ☐ **Side:** 8 gallon-size freezer baggie(s)

Freezer Meal Prep Day Shopping List by Recipe

Note: This shopping list doesn't include any side dish items like rice, dinner rolls, veggies or salad.
**In addition to a shopping list for prep day, this list could be used to help you organize ingredients on your counter before you begin preparing the meals for the freezer.

1. Baked Mexican Pork Chops

- ☐ 8 boneless pork chops
- ☐ 2 - 15 oz. can(s) corn
- ☐ 2 - 10 oz. cans diced tomatoes with green chilies
- ☐ 2 Tbsp ground cumin
- ☐ 2 tsp garlic powder
- ☐ Salt and pepper
- ☐ 2 cup(s) shredded Pepperjack cheese
- ☐ 2 - 9x13 disposable foil tray(s)

2. Slow Cooker Baja Shredded Chicken Tacos

- ☐ 6 large boneless chicken breasts
- ☐ 1/2 cup(s) brown sugar
- ☐ 2 Tbsp cumin
- ☐ 2/3 cup(s) salsa
- ☐ 2 - 4 oz. can(s) green chiles
- ☐ Salt and pepper
- ☐ 2 gallon-size freezer baggie(s)

3. Slow Cooker Pepperoni Chicken

- ☐ 8 small boneless chicken breasts
- ☐ 3 cup(s) pizza sauce
- ☐ 40 pepperonis
- ☐ 2 cup(s) shredded mozzarella cheese
- ☐ Salt and pepper
- ☐ 2 gallon-size freezer baggie(s)

4. Slow Cooker Teriyaki Chicken

- ☐ 6 large boneless chicken breasts
- ☐ Salt and pepper
- ☐ 2 - 12 oz. bags julienned carrots
- ☐ 4 cup(s) teriyaki sauce
- ☐ 2 gallon-size freezer baggie(s)

5. Slow Cooker Tomato Basil Tortellini Soup

- ☐ 2 - 26 oz. jar(s) spaghetti sauce
- ☐ 2 - 20 oz. box(es) of cheese tortellini
- ☐ 2 - 8 oz. box(es) sliced mushrooms
- ☐ 2 - 6 oz. bag(s) fresh spinach
- ☐ 8 fresh basil leaves
- ☐ 2 Tbsp minced onion
- ☐ 2 tsp minced garlic
- ☐ 8 cup(s) vegetable stock
- ☐ Salt and pepper
- ☐ 2 gallon-size freezer baggie(s)

Freezer Meal Prep Day Shopping List by Store Section/Category

Note: This shopping list doesn't include any side dish items like fruit, dinner rolls, veggies or salad.

Meat

- ☐ 8 boneless pork chops
- ☐ 12 large boneless chicken breasts
- ☐ 8 small boneless chicken breasts

Produce

- ☐ 2 - 12 oz. julienned carrots
- ☐ 2 - 8 oz. box(es) sliced mushrooms
- ☐ 2 - 6 oz. bag(s) fresh spinach
- ☐ 8 fresh basil leaves

Pantry Staples - Canned, Boxed

- ☐ 2 - 15 oz. can(s) corn
- ☐ 2 - 10 oz. cans diced tomatoes with green chilies
- ☐ 2/3 cup(s) salsa
- ☐ 2 - 4 oz. can(s) green chiles
- ☐ 8 cup(s) vegetable stock

Sauces/Condiments

- ☐ 3 cup(s) pizza sauce
- ☐ 4 cup(s) teriyaki sauce
- ☐ 2 - 26 oz. jar(s) spaghetti sauce

Spices

- ☐ 2 Tbsp ground cumin
- ☐ 2 tsp garlic powder
- ☐ Salt and pepper
- ☐ 1/2 cup(s) brown sugar
- ☐ 2 Tbsp cumin
- ☐ 40 pepperonis
- ☐ 2 Tbsp minced onion
- ☐ 2 tsp minced garlic

Dairy/Frozen

- ☐ 2 cup(s) shredded Pepperjack cheese
- ☐ 2 cup(s) shredded mozzarella cheese
- ☐ 2 - 20 oz. box(es) of cheese tortellini

Supplies

- ☐ 2 - 9x13 disposable foil tray(s)
- ☐ 8 gallon-size freezer baggie(s)

Meal Assembly Instructions

- ☐ Label your bags/foil with printable labels or sharpie.
- ☐ Pull out all the ingredients into a central location or into stations.

Pre-Cook & Chop Instructions

- ☐ Open and drain 2 cans of corn. Open and drain 2 cans of diced tomatoes with green chilies.
- ☐ In a mixing bowl, toss together the corn and diced tomatoes with green chilies with 2 Tbsp cumin and 2 tsp garlic powder.
- ☐ Open 2 cans of green chiles.

The Assembly Prep should take between 30 to 35 minutes.

Assembly by Recipe (Set Out on the Counter)

If you prefer to load your freezer baggies and trays one recipe at a time, you can follow the below instructions.

Baked Mexican Pork Chops

To each disposable tray, add the following ingredients:

- 4 boneless pork chops
- Half of the corn-tomatoes mixture over the pork chops
- Do not add the shredded cheese at the time of freezing

Cover with foil or lid, add label and freeze.

Slow Cooker Baja Shredded Chicken Tacos

To each gallon-size plastic freezer baggie, add the following ingredients:

- 3 large boneless chicken breasts
- 1/4 cup brown sugar
- 1 Tbsp cumin
- 1/3 cup salsa
- Half of the canned green chiles
- Salt and pepper

Remove as much air as possible and seal. Add label to baggie and freeze.

Slow Cooker Pepperoni Chicken

To each gallon-size plastic freezer baggie, add the following ingredients:

- 4 boneless chicken breasts
- 1 1/2 cups pizza sauce
- 20 pepperonis

Remove as much air as possible and seal. Add label to baggie and freeze.

Slow Cooker Teriyaki Chicken

To each gallon-size plastic freezer baggie, add the following ingredients:

- 3 large boneless, skinless chicken breasts
- Salt and pepper
- 12 oz. julienned carrots or "matchstick" carrots
- 2 cups teriyaki sauce
- Note: Do NOT add cornstarch to the freezer bag.

Remove as much as air as possible and seal.

Slow Cooker Tomato Basil Tortellini Soup

To each gallon-size plastic freezer baggie, add the following ingredients:

- 1 - 26 oz. jar spaghetti sauce
- 1 - 20 oz. box cheese tortellini
- 8 oz. sliced mushrooms
- 6 oz. fresh spinach
- 4 fresh basil leaves
- 1 Tbsp minced onion
- 1 tsp minced garlic
- 4 cups vegetable stock
- Salt and pepper

Remove as much air as possible and seal. Add label to baggie and freeze.

Freezer Meal Plan #2 - Recipes, Shopping Lists & Instructions

BBQ Chicken Street Tacos

Balsamic & Brown Sugar Pulled Pork

Cheesy Garlic Pork Chops

Slow Cooker Asian Shredded Beef

Slow Cooker Cheesy Salsa Chicken

Note: The following meal plans are written with 5 recipes that double to make a total of 10 meals. The shopping lists and instructions are written to make 2 meals worth of each recipe.

1. BBQ Chicken Street Tacos

Yield: 4 servings
Active Time: 10 minutes. Cook Time: 8 hours in slow cooker

Recipe is written to make a single meal. Assembly Prep Directions & Shopping Lists will both contain directions and ingredients to make 2 meals, based on the number of servings you selected.

** This ingredient is used on the day you cook this meal. It is not added at the time you assemble and prepare your meals for the freezer.

Ingredients for Single Meal

- 4 - small boneless chicken breasts
- 2 - cup(s) BBQ sauce
- 1 - 15 oz. can(s) black beans
- 1 small red onion(s)
- 12 - corn tortillas**
- Garnish: - shredded cheddar cheese
- Garnish: - chopped cilantro
- Side: - fruit**
- 1 - gallon-size freezer baggie(s)

Cooking Directions for Single Meal

1. Chop the red onion.
2. Open, drain and rinse the can(s) of black beans.
3. Spray bottom of slow cooker with cooking spray. Add the chicken breasts, black beans, red onions and pour the BBQ sauce over the top. Add about 1/4 to 1/2 cup of water to thin out the sauce.
4. Set the slow cooker on low and cook for 8 hours. Once cooked, shred the chicken into the BBQ sauce. Spoon shredded chicken and sauce into the corn tortillas and top with garnishes.
5. Prepare fruit and garnishes.
6. Serve BBQ Chicken Street Tacos with side of fruit.

Assembly Prep Directions for 2 Meals

- Chop 2 red onions.
- Open, drain and rinse 2 cans of black beans.
- To each gallon-size plastic freezer baggie, add the following ingredients:
  - 4 small boneless chicken breasts
  - 1 - 15 oz. can black beans
  - Half of the chopped red onion
  - 2 cups BBQ sauce
- Remove as much air as possible and seal. Add label to baggie and freeze.

Freeze & Thaw Instructions: *Put baggie in the freezer and freeze up to 6 months in fridge freezer or 12 months in a deep freezer. Thaw in the fridge overnight, or a warm bowl of water for about 20 minutes, before adding contents of the baggie to the slow cooker with amount of water listed in the recipe. Set on low and cook for 8 hours. Shred the chicken and make tacos.*

Dairy-Free Modifications: *Recipe is dairy-free when shredded cheese garnish is omitted.*

Gluten-Free Modifications: *Recipe is gluten-free when served with gluten-free sides.*

2. Balsamic & Brown Sugar Pulled Pork

Yield: 4 servings
Active Time: 5 minutes. Cook Time: 8 hours in slow cooker

Recipe is written to make a single meal. Assembly Prep Directions & Shopping Lists will both contain directions and ingredients to make 2 meals, based on the number of servings you selected.

** This ingredient is used on the day you cook this meal. It is not added at the time you assemble and prepare your meals for the freezer.

Ingredients for Single Meal

- 2 - lb(s) pork roast
- \- Salt and pepper
- 1/4 - cup(s) brown sugar
- 2 - Tbsp minced onion
- 1 - tsp garlic powder
- 1/4 - cup(s) balsamic vinegar
- Side: - fruit**
- Side: - potato chips**
- 1 - gallon-size freezer baggie(s)

Cooking Directions for Single Meal

1. In a small bowl, whisk together the brown sugar, minced onion, garlic powder and balsamic vinegar.
2. Place the pork roast into the base of the slow cooker and season with salt and pepper. Pour the sauce on and around the pork.
3. Set the slow cooker on low and cook for 8 hours. Once finished cooking, shred the pork with 2 forks and mix into the sauce. Strain before serving.
4. Prepare fruit.
5. Serve Balsamic & Brown Sugar Pulled Pork with chips and fruit.

Assembly Prep Directions for 2 Meals

- To each gallon-size plastic freezer baggie, add the following ingredients:
  - 2 lb. pork roast
  - Salt and pepper
  - 1/4 cup brown sugar
  - 2 Tbsp minced onion
  - 1 tsp garlic powder
  - 1/4 cup balsamic vinegar
- Remove as much air as possible and seal. Add label to baggie and freeze.

Freeze & Thaw Instructions: *Put baggie in the freezer and freeze up to 6 months in fridge freezer or 12 months in a deep freezer. Thaw in the fridge overnight, or a warm bowl of water for about 20 minutes, before transferring to the slow cooker and cooking on low for 8 hours.*

Special Notes: *Substitute balsamic glaze for the balsamic vinegar for a thicker sauce.*

Dairy-Free Modifications: *Recipe is dairy-free when served with dairy-free sides.*

Gluten-Free Modifications: *Recipe is gluten-free when served with gluten-free sides.*

3. Cheesy Garlic Pork Chops

Yield: 4 servings
Active Time: 5 minutes. Cook Time: 35 minutes

Recipe is written to make a single meal. Assembly Prep Directions & Shopping Lists will both contain directions and ingredients to make 2 meals, based on the number of servings you selected.

** This ingredient is used on the day you cook this meal. It is not added at the time you assemble and prepare your meals for the freezer.

Ingredients for Single Meal

- 4 - boneless pork chops
- - Salt and pepper
- 2 - Tbsp melted butter
- 2 - tsp minced garlic
- 1 - tsp onion powder
- 1 - cup(s) shredded mild cheddar cheese
- Side: - dinner rolls**
- Side: - veggies**
- 1 - 9x13 disposable foil tray(s)

Cooking Directions for Single Meal

1. Preheat the oven to 350 F. Lightly spray a 9x13-inch baking dish with non-stick cooking spray. Place the pork chops into the baking dish and season with salt and pepper.
2. In a small bowl, stir the melted butter, minced garlic, and onion powder. Brush it onto the pork chops. Add a few pinchfuls of shredded mild cheddar cheese onto each pork chops.
3. Bake in the preheated oven for 25 to 35 minutes, or until pork chops reach 145 F. Let rest for 5 minutes before serving or slicing. Cooking time may vary depending on thickness of the pork chops.
4. Prepare veggies.
5. Warm the dinner rolls.
6. Serve Cheesy Garlic Pork Chops with veggies and dinner rolls.

Assembly Prep Directions for 2 Meals

- In a small bowl, stir 4 Tbsp melted butter, 4 tsp minced garlic, and 2 tsp onion powder.
- To each disposable tray, add the following ingredients:
  - 4 boneless pork chops
  - Melted butter mixture, brushed onto each pork chop
  - Pinchfuls of shredded mild cheddar, onto each pork chop
- Cover with foil or lid, add label and freeze.

Freeze & Thaw Instructions: *Put tray in the freezer and freeze up to 6 months in fridge freezer or 12 months in a deep freezer. Thaw in the fridge overnight, or a shallow dish of warm water for about 20 minutes, before transferring to the oven and baking as directed.*

Dairy-Free Modifications: *Unfortunately, there isn't a great dairy-free option for this meal.*

Gluten-Free Modifications: *Recipe is gluten-free when served with gluten-free sides.*

4. Slow Cooker Asian Shredded Beef

Yield: 4 servings
Active Time: 10 minutes. Cook Time: 8 hours in slow cooker

Recipe is written to make a single meal. Assembly Prep Directions & Shopping Lists will both contain directions and ingredients to make 2 meals, based on the number of servings you selected.

** This ingredient is used on the day you cook this meal. It is not added at the time you assemble and prepare your meals for the freezer.

Ingredients for Single Meal

- 2 - lb(s) beef chuck roast
- - Salt and pepper
- 1/3 - cup(s) hoisin sauce
- 1/3 - cup(s) soy sauce
- 2 - Tbsp rice vinegar
- 2 - Tbsp honey
- 1 - Tbsp sesame oil
- 1 - tsp ground ginger
- 1 - tsp crushed red pepper
- Garnish: - sliced green onions**
- Side: - rice**
- Side: - veggies**
- 1 - gallon-size freezer baggie(s)

Cooking Directions for Single Meal

1. Place the beef roast into the base of the slow cooker and season with salt and pepper.
2. In a mixing bowl, whisk together the hoisin sauce, soy sauce, rice vinegar, honey, sesame oil, ginger and crushed red pepper.
3. Pour the sauce over the beef in the slow cooker.
4. Set the slow cooker on low and cook for 8 hours. Once finished cooking, shred the beef with 2 forks and mix into the sauce.
5. Cook the rice, as directed.
6. Prepare the veggies.
7. Serve Slow Cooker Asian Shredded Beef over rice with veggies and green onion garnish.

Assembly Prep Directions for 2 Meals

- In a mixing bowl, whisk together 2/3 cup hoisin sauce, 2/3 cup soy sauce, 4 Tbsp rice vinegar, 4 Tbsp honey, 2 Tbsp sesame oil, 2 tsp ground ginger and 2 tsp crushed red pepper.
- To each gallon-size plastic freezer baggie, add the following ingredients:
  - 2 lb. beef chuck roast
  - Salt and pepper
  - Half of the prepared sauce
- Remove as much air as possible and seal. Add label to baggie and freeze.

Freeze & Thaw Instructions: Put baggie in the freezer and freeze up to 6 months in fridge freezer or 12 months in a deep freezer. Thaw in the fridge overnight, or a warm bowl of water for about 20 minutes, before transferring to the slow cooker and cooking on low for 8 hours. Shred the beef before serving.

Dairy-Free Modifications: Recipe is dairy-free when served with dairy-free sides.

Gluten-Free Modifications: Recipe is gluten-free when you make it with gluten-free soy sauce and hoisin sauce.

5. Slow Cooker Cheesy Salsa Chicken

Yield: 4 servings
Active Time: 10 minutes. Cook Time: 8 hours in slow cooker

Recipe is written to make a single meal. Assembly Prep Directions & Shopping Lists will both contain directions and ingredients to make 2 meals, based on the number of servings you selected.

** This ingredient is used on the day you cook this meal. It is not added at the time you assemble and prepare your meals for the freezer.

Ingredients for Single Meal

- 4 - small boneless chicken breasts
- 1 - cup(s) red salsa
- 2 - Tbsp taco seasoning
- 1/2 - cup(s) sour cream**
- 2 - cup(s) shredded cheese**
- - Salt and pepper
- Side: - rice**
- Side: - salad**
- 1 - gallon-size freezer baggie(s)

Cooking Directions for Single Meal

1. Place the chicken breasts in the base of the slow cooker and pour the red salsa and taco seasoning over and around the chicken. (Note: Do not add the sour cream before slow cooking.)
2. Set on low and cook for 8 hours. With 30 minutes, left in the cooking cycle, stir in the sour cream and let finish cooking. Once finished cooking, add the shredded cheese on top and let melt. Season with salt and pepper to taste.
3. Cook the rice as directed.
4. Prepare the salad.
5. Serve Slow Cooker Cheesy Salsa Chicken with shredded cheese garnish over rice with salad.

Assembly Prep Directions for 2 Meals

- To each gallon-size plastic freezer baggie, add the following ingredients:
  - 4 boneless chicken breasts
  - 1 cup red salsa
  - 2 Tbsp taco seasoning
  - Do NOT add the sour cream or shredded cheese
  - before freezing.
- Remove as much air as possible and seal. Add label to baggie and freeze.

Freeze & Thaw Instructions: *Put baggie in the freezer and freeze up to 6 months in fridge freezer or 12 months in a deep freezer. Thaw in the fridge overnight, or a warm bowl of water for about 20 minutes, before transferring to the slow cooker and cooking on low for 8 hours. Stir in the sour cream at the end of the cooking cycle as directed. Top with shredded cheese, once finished cooking.*

Dairy-Free Modifications: *Unfortunately, there is not a great dairy-free option for this meal.*

Gluten-Free Modifications: *Recipe is gluten-free when served with gluten-free sides.*

Complete Shopping List by Recipe

1. BBQ Chicken Street Tacos

- ☐ 8 small boneless chicken breasts
- ☐ 4 cup(s) BBQ sauce
- ☐ 2 - 15 oz. can(s) black beans
- ☐ 1 small red onion
- ☐ 24 corn tortillas
- ☐ **Garnish:** shredded cheddar cheese
- ☐ **Garnish:** chopped cilantro
- ☐ **Side:** fruit
- ☐ 2 gallon-size freezer baggie(s)

2. Balsamic & Brown Sugar Pulled Pork

- ☐ 4 lb(s) pork roast
- ☐ Salt and pepper
- ☐ 1/2 cup(s) brown sugar
- ☐ 4 Tbsp minced onion
- ☐ 2 tsp garlic powder
- ☐ 1/2 cup(s) balsamic vinegar
- ☐ **Side:** fruit
- ☐ **Side:** potato chips
- ☐ 2 - gallon-size freezer baggie(s)

3. Cheesy Garlic Pork Chops

- ☐ 8 boneless pork chops
- ☐ Salt and pepper
- ☐ 4 Tbsp melted butter
- ☐ 4 tsp minced garlic
- ☐ 2 tsp onion powder
- ☐ 2 cup(s) shredded mild cheddar cheese
- ☐ **Side:** dinner rolls
- ☐ **Side:** veggies
- ☐ 2 - 9x13 disposable foil tray(s)

4. Slow Cooker Asian Shredded Beef

- ☐ 4 lb(s) beef chuck roast
- ☐ Salt and pepper
- ☐ 2/3 cup(s) hoisin sauce
- ☐ 2/3 cup(s) soy sauce
- ☐ 4 Tbsp rice vinegar
- ☐ 4 Tbsp honey
- ☐ 2 Tbsp sesame oil
- ☐ 2 tsp ground ginger
- ☐ 2 tsp crushed red pepper
- ☐ sliced green onions
- ☐ **Side:** rice
- ☐ **Side:** veggies
- ☐ 2 gallon-size freezer baggie(s)

5. Slow Cooker Cheesy Salsa Chicken

- ☐ 8 small boneless chicken breasts
- ☐ 2 cup(s) red salsa
- ☐ 4 Tbsp taco seasoning
- ☐ 1 cup(s) sour cream
- ☐ 2 cup(s) shredded cheese
- ☐ Salt and pepper
- ☐ **Side:** rice
- ☐ **Side:** salad
- ☐ 2 gallon-size freezer baggie(s)

Complete Shopping List by Store Section/Category

Meat

- [ ] 16 small boneless chicken breasts
- [ ] 4 lb(s) pork roast
- [ ] 8 boneless pork chops
- [ ] 4 lb(s) beef chuck roast

Produce

- [ ] 2 small red onions(s)
- [ ] **Garnish:** chopped cilantro
- [ ] **Side:** fruit
- [ ] **Side:** veggies
- [ ] **Garnish:** sliced green onions
- [ ] **Side:** salad

Pantry Staples - Canned, Boxed

- [ ] 2 - 15 oz. can(s) black beans
- [ ] **Side:** rice
- [ ] 2 cup(s) red salsa

Starchy Sides

- [ ] 24 corn tortillas
- [ ] **Side:** potato chips
- [ ] **Side:** dinner rolls

Sauces/Condiments

- [ ] 4 cup(s) BBQ sauce
- [ ] 1/2 cup(s) balsamic vinegar
- [ ] 2/3 cup(s) hoisin sauce
- [ ] 2/3 cup(s) soy sauce
- [ ] 4 Tbsp rice vinegar
- [ ] 4 Tbsp honey
- [ ] 2 Tbsp sesame oil

Spices

- [ ] Salt and pepper
- [ ] 1/2 cup(s) brown sugar
- [ ] 4 Tbsp minced onion
- [ ] 2 tsp garlic powder
- [ ] 4 tsp minced garlic
- [ ] 2 tsp onion powder
- [ ] 2 tsp ground ginger
- [ ] 2 tsp crushed red pepper
- [ ] 4 Tbsp taco seasoning

Dairy/Frozen

- [ ] **Garnish:** shredded cheddar cheese
- [ ] 2 cup(s) shredded mild cheddar cheese
- [ ] 1 cup(s) sour cream
- [ ] 4 Tbsp melted butter
- [ ] **Side:** 2 cup(s) shredded cheese

Supplies

- [ ] **Side:** 8 gallon-size freezer baggie(s)
- [ ] **Side:** 2 - 9x13 disposable foil tray(s)

Freezer Meal Prep Day Shopping List by Recipe

Note: This shopping list doesn't include any side dish items like rice, dinner rolls, veggies or salad.
**In addition to a shopping list for prep day, this list could be used to help you organize ingredients on your counter before you begin preparing the meals for the freezer.

1. BBQ Chicken Street Tacos

- ☐ 8 small boneless chicken breasts
- ☐ 4 cup(s) BBQ sauce
- ☐ 2 - 15 oz. can(s) black beans
- ☐ 2 small red onions(s)
- ☐ 2 gallon-size freezer baggie(s)

2. Balsamic & Brown Sugar Pulled Pork

- ☐ 4 lb(s) pork roast
- ☐ Salt and pepper
- ☐ 1/2 cup(s) brown sugar
- ☐ 4 Tbsp minced onion
- ☐ 2 tsp garlic powder
- ☐ 1/2 cup(s) balsamic vinegar
- ☐ 2 gallon-size freezer baggie(s)

3. Cheesy Garlic Pork Chops

- ☐ 8 boneless pork chops
- ☐ Salt and pepper
- ☐ 4 Tbsp melted butter
- ☐ 4 tsp minced garlic
- ☐ 2 tsp onion powder
- ☐ 2 cup(s) shredded mild cheddar cheese
- ☐ 2 - 9x13 disposable foil tray(s)

4. Slow Cooker Asian Shredded Beef

- ☐ 4 lb(s) beef chuck roast
- ☐ Salt and pepper
- ☐ 2/3 cup(s) hoisin sauce
- ☐ 2/3 cup(s) soy sauce
- ☐ 4 Tbsp rice vinegar
- ☐ 4 Tbsp honey
- ☐ 2 Tbsp sesame oil
- ☐ 2 tsp ground ginger
- ☐ 2 tsp crushed red pepper
- ☐ 2 gallon-size freezer baggie(s)

5. Slow Cooker Cheesy Salsa Chicken

- ☐ 8 small boneless chicken breasts
- ☐ 2 cup(s) red salsa
- ☐ 4 Tbsp taco seasoning
- ☐ Salt and pepper
- ☐ 2 gallon-size freezer baggie(s)

Freezer Meal Prep Day Shopping List by Store Section/Category

Note: This shopping list doesn't include any side dish items like fruit, dinner rolls, veggies or salad.

Meat

- ☐ 16 small boneless chicken breasts
- ☐ 4 lb(s) pork roast
- ☐ 8 boneless pork chops
- ☐ 4 lb(s) beef chuck roast

Produce

- ☐ 2 small red onions(s)

Pantry Staples - Canned, Boxed

- ☐ 2 - 15 oz. can(s) black beans
- ☐ 2 cup(s) red salsa

Sauces/Condiments

- ☐ 4 cup(s) BBQ sauce
- ☐ 1/2 cup(s) balsamic vinegar
- ☐ 2/3 cup(s) hoisin sauce
- ☐ 2/3 cup(s) soy sauce
- ☐ 4 Tbsp rice vinegar
- ☐ 4 Tbsp honey
- ☐ 2 Tbsp sesame oil

Spices

- ☐ Salt and pepper
- ☐ 1/2 cup(s) brown sugar
- ☐ 4 Tbsp minced onion
- ☐ 2 tsp garlic powder
- ☐ 4 tsp minced garlic
- ☐ 2 tsp onion powder
- ☐ 2 tsp ground ginger
- ☐ 2 tsp crushed red pepper
- ☐ 4 Tbsp taco seasoning

Dairy/Frozen

- ☐ 2 cup(s) shredded mild cheddar cheese
- ☐ 4 Tbsp melted butter

Supplies

- ☐ 8 gallon-size freezer baggie(s)
- ☐ 2 - 9x13 disposable foil tray(s)

Meal Assembly Instructions

- ☐ Label your bags/foil with printable labels or sharpie.
- ☐ Pull out all the ingredients into a central location or into stations.

Pre-Cook & Chop Instructions

- ☐ Chop 2 red onions.
- ☐ In a mixing bowl, whisk together 2/3 cup hoisin sauce, 2/3 cup soy sauce, 4 Tbsp rice vinegar, 4 Tbsp honey, 2 Tbsp sesame oil, 2 tsp ground ginger and 2 tsp crushed red pepper.
- ☐ In a small bowl, stir 4 Tbsp melted butter, 4 tsp minced garlic, and 2 tsp onion powder.
- ☐ Open, drain and rinse 2 cans of black beans.

The Assembly Prep should take between 30 to 35 minutes.

Assembly by Recipe (Set Out on the Counter)

If you prefer to load your freezer baggies and trays one recipe at a time, you can follow the below instructions.

BBQ Chicken Street Tacos

To each gallon-size plastic freezer baggie, add the following ingredients:

- 4 small boneless chicken breasts
- 1 - 15 oz. can black beans
- Half of the chopped red onion
- 2 cups BBQ sauce

Remove as much air as possible and seal. Add label to baggie and freeze.

Balsamic & Brown Sugar Pulled Pork

To each gallon-size plastic freezer baggie, add the following ingredients:

- 2 lb. pork roast
- Salt and pepper
- 1/4 cup brown sugar
- 2 Tbsp minced onion
- 1 tsp garlic powder
- 1/4 cup balsamic vinegar

Remove as much air as possible and seal. Add label to baggie and freeze.

Cheesy Garlic Pork Chops

To each disposable tray, add the following ingredients:

- 4 boneless pork chops
- Melted butter mixture, brushed onto each pork chop
- Pinchfuls of shredded mild cheddar, onto each pork chop

Cover with foil or lid, add label and freeze.

Slow Cooker Asian Shredded Beef

To each gallon-size plastic freezer baggie, add the following ingredients:

- 2 lb. beef chuck roast
- Salt and pepper
- Half of the prepared sauce

Remove as much air as possible and seal. Add label to baggie and freeze.

Slow Cooker Cheesy Salsa Chicken

To each gallon-size plastic freezer baggie, add the following ingredients:

- 4 boneless chicken breasts
- 1 cup red salsa
- 2 Tbsp taco seasoning
- Do NOT add the sour cream or shredded cheese before freezing.

Remove as much air as possible and seal. Add label to baggie and freeze.

Freezer Cooking Resources
from Erin Chase

Let's Connect

Hi friend! Need more help or inspiration on your freezer cooking journey? Come join our group on Facebook - it's basically a "freezer cooking hotline" and an amazing, supportive community.
Visit https://bit.ly/MyFrEZFB to join the group.

Join MyFreezEasy

Freezer Meal Cookbooks

Freezer Meal Plan PDFs

Made in United States
Troutdale, OR
07/01/2025

32548146R00058